# HAZARDOUS SUBSTANCES
## a reference

## MELVIN BERGER

ENSLOW PUBLISHERS, INC.

Bloy St. & Ramsey Ave.     P.O. Box 38
Box 777     Aldershot
Hillside, N.J. 07205    Hants GU12 6BP
U.S.A.     U.K.

The author thanks the following persons for reviewing
the manuscript for scientific accuracy:

Dr. Howard Beim
Professor of Chemistry
U.S. Merchant Marine Academy

Dr. George M. Hoerner, Jr.
Chairman, Dept. of Chemical Engineering
Lafayette College

**Library of Congress Cataloging in Publication Data**

Berger, Melvin.
    Hazardous substances, a reference.

    Bibliography: p.
    1. Poisons—Dictionaries. 2. Hazardous substances—
Dictionaries. I. Title. [DNLM: 1. Environmental Exposure—handbooks. 2. Environmental Exposure—popular
works. 3. Environmental Pollutants—handbooks. 4. Environmental Pollutants—popular works. WA 39 B496h]
RA1193.B475      1986      363.1'79      86-8806
ISBN 0-89490-116-8

Printed in the United States of America

10 9 8 7 6 5 4 3 2 1

# CONTENTS

# INTRODUCTION

Hazardous substances are all around us—in the air we breathe, the water we drink, the food we eat, the clothes we wear. We are exposed to them in our homes, stores, schools, factories, offices, cars, and outdoors as well. Sometimes we can see and feel them as solids or liquids. Other times we can smell them as gases.

All hazardous substances are the same in one way: They make us sick or cause some harm to the human body. Many of the substances result in temporary illness, such as headache, nausea, or dizziness. Several lead to serious, permanent conditions that range from kidney or liver damage to cancer. And a few are so poisonous that even a brief exposure may result in death.

*Hazardous Substances: A Reference* is a complete, dictionary-like guide to more than 230 dangerous materials in the environment. Included are substances as well as other environmental hazards, such as radiation, heat, and noise, that affect the largest number of people, that are the most toxic, and that receive the greatest attention from the media. Separate entries identify each environmental hazard, describe how and where it is used, and discuss its effects on exposed individuals. There are also accounts of several of the most notorious hazardous substance disasters of modern times, such as those at Bhopal, India; Love Canal, New York; and Times Beach, Missouri.

The information on each hazardous substance takes in the following:

**Name.** The most common term for the hazardous substance is given at the beginning of each entry.

**Acronym.** A substance is often known by the first letters of the words or syllables that make up its chemical name. If a substance has a frequently used acronym, it appears right after the substance name.

**Formula.** The composition of the substance is represented by the standard chemical symbol or symbols. Among the symbols that appear most frequently are C (carbon), H (hydrogen), O (oxygen), Cl (chlorine), S (sulfur), K (potassium), and P (phosphorus). The subscript ($O_2$ for example) shows how many atoms of each element are found in a molecule of the substance.

**Description.** Each of the hazardous substances has its own appearance and characteristics. The ones that are mentioned are state (solid, liquid, or gas), color, smell, texture, and flammability.

**Standard.** OSHA (Occupational Safety and Health Administration) has adopted legal standards, or limits, for exposure to most of the hazardous substances. The numbers show the maximum amount of the substance a person may be exposed to for eight hours a day over a typical working career with no bad effect. They are known as the Threshold Limit Value-Time Weighted Average (TLV-TWA). The OSHA figures are given either in parts per billion (ppb), parts per million (ppm), or milligrams per cubic meter ($mg/m^3$). (See Terms Used in the Field for definitions of these terms.) Sometimes other groups (the Environmental Protection Agency, etc.) also publish lists of limits for chemicals not on the OSHA list.

**Uses.** The materials have a wide variety of purposes and applications. They vary from being present in everyone's daily life to being part of special industrial processes. In addition, some substances are the result of the production of other desired materials.

**Health effects.** Exposure to a hazardous substance often results in either short- or long-range symptoms and illnesses.

Quite frequently the victim does not even associate the health problem with exposure.

**Other names.** Some hazardous substances are known by more than one name. These less common names are also listed alphabetically, where they direct the reader to the main entry.

**References.** For those seeking more information on particular substances, numbers in parentheses at the end of the entries are keyed to the books or pamphlets in the References section. For further details on all the substances, consult the three most complete sources: National Institute for Occupational Safety and Health, *Registry of Toxic Effects of Chemical Substances;* Sax and Feiner, *Dangerous Properties of Industrial Materials;* and Sittig, *Handbook of Toxic and Hazardous Chemicals.*

The basic information in *Hazardous Substances: A Reference* was gathered from a wide variety of up-to-date research sources. The formulas and standards were compiled from the *Register of Toxic Effects of Chemical Sources,* published in 1983 by the National Institute for Occupational Safety and Health of the United States Department of Health and Human Services.

In addition to the separate entries on the hazardous substances, which make up the body of *Hazardous Substances: A Reference*, there are four other sections:

**Federal Laws and Agencies.** Brief descriptions of the various federal laws and government agencies that deal with toxic substances.

**References.** A listing of books and pamphlets for further reading.

**Terms Used in the Field.** Definitions of the special terms associated with hazardous substances and their effects.

**For Further Information.** The addresses of the government agencies and public interest organizations that can furnish more information on hazardous substances.

# TERMS USED IN THE FIELD

**ACUTE.** When referring to disease it means one that is severe and brief, not long-lasting or chronic; also used to describe a short exposure to a hazardous substance.

**AGENCY.** A department or division of the government that is responsible for administering or carrying out some particular legislation. The Environmental Protection Agency (EPA) and Occupational Safety and Health Administration (OSHA) are examples of federal agencies involved with hazardous substance legislation.

**ANOREXIA.** The loss of appetite in which the individual stops eating or eats much less.

**ANTIOXIDANT.** A chemical substance that prevents materials from becoming rancid or spoiled, or from developing discoloration and offensive odors.

**ASPHYXIA.** Suffocation from lack of air.

**BIRTH DEFECTS.** Inherited disorders that affect babies. Some birth defects are passed on through faulty genes. Others result from the action of some environmental factor on the genes. Still others are the outcome of an unsatisfactory prenatal environment.

**BY-PRODUCT.** A substance that is produced incidentally during the manufacture or processing of another substance; also called co-product.

**CANCER.** Harmful growth or tumor in the body that tends to spread and destroy healthy tissue and organs. Over 400,000 people die each year from cancer. Estimates of the number of these cancer deaths caused per year by exposure to toxic chemicals range from about 20,000 to 80,000. In 1982, the National Toxic Program reported a minimum of 116 chemicals or processes that might cause cancer in humans. The costs of cancer, in terms of medical care and lost productivity, total an estimated $30 billion a year.

**CARCINOGEN.** Any substance that can cause cancer. Scientists have three basic ways to determine whether something is a carcinogen: epidemiologic studies to see if people who are exposed to the substance develop more cancers than the general population; experimental animal studies to see the effect of inhaling, ingesting, or making contact with the substance; and in vitro research to observe the effect of the substance on cells or bacteria growing in test tubes.

**CENTRAL NERVOUS SYSTEM.** The part of the nervous system consisting of the brain and spinal cord.

**CHEMICAL.** Any substance that is either an element (kind of atom), a compound (molecule, or combination of two or more atoms), or a mixture (a nonbinding combination of two or more substances).

**CHRONIC.** When referring to disease it means one that lasts a long time or recurs frequently; also used to describe extended exposure to a hazardous substance, usually at a low level.

**CODE OF FEDERAL REGULATIONS.** A series of publications that contain the regulations put into effect by the various governmental agencies.

**COMA.** A deep, long-lasting unconsciousness usually caused by injury, disease, or poison.

**CO-PRODUCT.** See **BY-PRODUCT.**

**CONTAMINATE.** To make impure or to pollute by contact or by mixing.

**CONVULSIONS.** Involuntary movements of the whole body or of some part.

**CORROSIVE.** A material that wears away the surface of a substance by chemical action. Also the description of such a material.

**CUMULATIVE POISON.** A class of toxic substances that is not eliminated by normal body processes. Thus, continued exposure results in a gradual build-up to damaging levels.

**DELIRIUM.** A temporary mental disturbance resulting from high fever, intoxication, or shock. The symptoms may include confusion, uncontrolled shaking, hallucinations, and incoherent speech.

**DERMATITIS.** Inflammation of the skin.

**DIARRHEA.** The frequent passage of loose and watery stools.

**EDEMA.** Swelling caused by the accumulation of fluids in

tissues of the body. Edema can usually be noticed first on the ankles or around the lower back.

**EPIDEMIOLOGY.** The study of diseases as they affect large numbers of people rather than individuals.

**EXPOSURE.** Coming in contact with something, such as a hazardous substance, and being subjected to its influence. See also **ACUTE** and **CHRONIC.**

**FLAMMABLE.** The ability of a substance to burn. See also **IGNITION.**

**FUMIGANT.** A substance that kills vermin or insects by exposing them to irritating smoke, gas, or vapor.

**FUNGICIDE.** A substance that kills fungi, including yeasts, molds, mildews, and mushrooms, or prevents their growth.

**HALF-LIFE.** The average time required for half the atoms in a sample of a radioactive substance to lose their radioactivity by decaying into other atoms.

**HAZARD.** Something that is likely to have an adverse effect on humans, the environment, or property.

**HAZARDOUS SUBSTANCES.** Materials that pose a threat to human health or to other living organisms, or that may cause property damage through fire, explosion, etc. There are an estimated 27,000 such materials in commercial use. About 25 million workers (one out of every four Americans) are exposed to hazardous substances.

**HAZARDOUS WASTES.** Discarded material that may cause or significantly contribute to serious illness or death. The

United States generates about 80 million tons of hazardous wastes a year. See **BY-PRODUCT**.

**HERBICIDE.** A substance for killing undesirable plants, especially weeds.

**IGNITION.** Providing sufficient energy to a flammable material so that it starts to burn.

**INSECTICIDE.** A substance used for killing insects.

**INSOMNIA.** The inability to fall asleep or to get enough sleep.

**LD50.** See **LETHAL DOSE**.

**LATENT.** Hidden or waiting to develop. Cancer, for example, has a long period of latency between exposure and the first appearance of symptoms. Those forms of cancer induced by chemical substances are believed to have a latency period of about twenty years.

**LAW.** A rule or body of rules put forth by a governing body, such as the United States Congress, which is legally binding. Also a statement of a chemical or physical principle.

**LEACHATE.** Water that has been filtered or forced through hazardous wastes, and may have become contaminated as a result.

**LETHAL DOSE.** A measure of the amount of a substance that is fatal to a living being in an acute exposure. The lethal dose may be shown as LD50. That is the amount that will kill 50 percent of the experimental animals. More often now the lethal dose is expressed as the amount of the substance per unit of body weight that will be fatal.

**MISCARRIAGE.** The birth of a fetus before it is able to survive outside the uterus. Most miscarriages occur between the fourth and seventh months of pregnancy.

**MUTAGEN.** Any substance that brings about changes in the genes or chromosomes of plants and animals, causing different characteristics to appear in their offspring.

**M³** Cubic meter. A volume that measures one meter (39.37 inches) high by one meter deep by one meter across. It is equal to 35.31 cubic feet.

**MG.** Abbreviation for milligram or milligrams. A milligram is 1/1000 gram (0.001 gram), which is equal to 35/100,000 ounce (0.000035 ounce).

**MG/M³.** A commonly used standard. It expresses the number of allowable milligrams of a substance in a cubic meter of air. See also **M³** and **MG.**

**MONITORING.** Determining the level of pollution or radioactivity by periodic or continuous sampling.

**NARCOTIC.** A substance that produces sleep, dullness, or stupor, and also relieves pain.

**NAUSEA.** The sick feeling in the stomach that is usually followed by vomiting. The person will often look pale and sweaty.

**NEMATOCIDE.** A substance that kills different kinds of worms.

**NEPHRITIS.** Inflammation of the kidneys.

**PARANOIA.** A chronic mental disorder in which there are delusions, usually of persecution.

**PARTICULATES.** Solid particles or liquid droplets small enough to remain suspended in the air. Particulates can irritate the human respiratory system and cause lung disease. About two-thirds of the particulates in the environment are from industry, vehicles, and solid-waste disposal.

**PARTS PER BILLION.** A commonly used standard. It indicates the number of parts of a particular substance found in one billion parts of another substance, usually on the basis of weight.

**PARTS PER MILLION.** A commonly used standard. It indicates the number of parts of a particular substance found in one million parts of another substance, usually on the basis of weight.

**POLYMER.** A natural or synthetic compound consisting of a large number of similar molecules linked together.

**POLLUTION STANDARD INDEX.** A set of EPA levels based on the concentrations of five pollutants in the air: carbon monoxide, sulfur dioxide, total suspended particulates, ozone, and nitrogen dioxide. At a level of less than 100, no restrictions are needed; at 100-200, people with heart or respiratory disease should cut down on activity; at 300-400, all should reduce outdoor activity; and above 400, all should keep doors and windows shut with a minimum of physical activity.

**PPB.** See **PARTS PER BILLION.**

**PPM.** See **PARTS PER MILLION.**

**PSI.** See **POLLUTION STANDARD INDEX.**

**REACTIVITY.** The ability of a substance to combine chemically with another material. A high reactivity is usually a reason for classifying a material as hazardous.

**REGULATION.** A rule put forth by a government agency or department, such as the Environmental Protection Agency (EPA) or Occupational Safety and Health Administration (OSHA), to carry out the intent of the law. All regulations are published in the *Code of Federal Regulations*.

**RESPIRATION.** The act of breathing.

**RISK.** The chance of injury or loss based on hazard and exposure. As the danger of injury or loss approaches zero, so does the risk. It is based on the probability of the undesired event occurring, and the severity of the results if it does occur.

**STANDARD.** The maximum safe concentration of a hazardous substance, usually expressed in milligrams per cubic meter ($mg/m^3$), parts per million (ppm), or parts per billion (ppb). See also **MG/M$^3$**, **PARTS PER BILLION**, and **PARTS PER MILLION.**

**STRUCTURE-ACTIVITY RELATIONSHIP.** A theory that may one day be able to predict chemical toxicity. The process uses a computer to break down the molecules in a chemical of unknown toxicity into fragments called structural units. The fragments are then compared with a catalog of the structural units in known toxic substances. The more matches that are found, the more likely it is that the chemical should be considered toxic.

**TDS.** See **TOTAL DISSOLVED SOLIDS.**

**TERATOGEN.** Any substance that is suspected of causing serious deformities in the offspring of animals or plants. These changes from the normal are not inherited.

**TOLERANCE.** The ability of an organism to cope with changes in its environment. Also the safe level of any hazardous substance.

**TOTAL DISSOLVED SOLIDS (TDS).** A measure of the total of inorganic salts and other substances that is dissolved in water.

**TOXIC.** Poisonous. Any substance that presents an unreasonable risk of injury to health or the environment. See also **LETHAL DOSE.**

**TOXICITY.** The degree of danger posed by a substance to animal or plant life. See also **LETHAL DOSE.**

**VERTIGO.** Dizziness.

**VOMITING.** The forcible expulsion of stomach contents through the mouth.

# FEDERAL LAWS AND AGENCIES

**ACID PRECIPITATION ACT.** A federal law passed in 1980 establishing an Interagency Task Force on Acid Precipitation. One of its main purposes is to develop a ten-year research plan on acid rain.

**CERCLA.** See **COMPREHENSIVE ENVIRONMENTAL RESPONSE, COMPENSATION, AND LIABILITY ACT (1980).**

**CLEAN AIR ACT.** The broad, general law, first adopted in 1970, that strives to guarantee pure, clean air, free of toxic gases and particulates, for all Americans. It has been amended many times since the original law was passed.

**CLEAN WATER ACT.** The law passed by Congress in 1972 that has as its basic goal to put an end to "the discharge of toxic pollutants in toxic amounts" into our nation's water.

**COMPREHENSIVE ENVIRONMENTAL RESPONSE, COMPENSATION, AND LIABILITY ACT (1980) (CERCLA).** The law broadens federal responsibility and authority on the release of specified hazardous substances into the air, water, or ground. It authorizes the federal government (through the EPA) to respond directly to releases (or threatened releases) of hazardous substances that may endanger public health or welfare.

**CONSUMER PRODUCT SAFETY COMMISSION (CPSC).** A government agency that sets safety standards for consumer products. If the commission cannot devise an adequate standard it may ban a product.

**CPSC.** See **CONSUMER PRODUCT SAFETY COMMISSION.**

**ENVIRONMENTAL PROTECTION AGENCY (EPA).** An independent agency of the federal government formed in 1970. The EPA is responsible for pollution control programs that affect air, water, radiation, solid and toxic wastes, pesticides, and noise. (3)

**EPA.** See **ENVIRONMENTAL PROTECTION AGENCY.**

**FEDERAL ENVIRONMENTAL PESTICIDE CONTROL ACT (FEPCA)** . A law passed in 1947 and amended in 1972 that requires all manufacturers of pesticides to register their products with the EPA.

**FEDERAL HAZARDOUS SUBSTANCES ACT (FHSA).** Passed in 1960, the law prohibits the interstate shipment of hazardous substances without correct labels.

**FDA.** See **FOOD AND DRUG ADMINISTRATION.**

**FEPCA.** See **FEDERAL ENVIRONMENTAL PESTICIDE CONTROL ACT.**

**FHSA.** See **FEDERAL HAZARDOUS SUBSTANCES ACT.**

**FOOD AND DRUG ADMINISTRATION.** The federal agency responsible for monitoring the purity, effectiveness, labels, etc., of food, drugs, and cosmetics.

**NATIONAL INSTITUTE FOR OCCUPATIONAL SAFETY AND HEALTH (NIOSH).** A government agency that develops recommendations for limits of exposure to hazardous substances or conditions in the workplace. The agency also recommends preventive measures to reduce or eliminate the adverse health effects of hazardous substances.

**NATIONAL TOXICOLOGY PROGRAM (NTP).** A government project established in November 1978 to do research on hazardous substances, and to protect the population from the many dangerous chemicals in use in the United States. Of the 60,000 chemical substances currently available, the NTP has tested close to 2,000.

**NIOSH.** See **NATIONAL INSTITUTE FOR OCCUPATIONAL SAFETY AND HEALTH.**

**NTP.** See **NATIONAL TOXICOLOGY PROGRAM.**

**OCCUPATIONAL SAFETY AND HEALTH ACT.** The Act was passed in December 1970 to assure employees safe and healthful working conditions. It created the Occupational Safety and Health Administration (OSHA) to set standards for hazards in the work environment.

**OCCUPATIONAL SAFETY AND HEALTH ADMINISTRATION (OSHA).** The agency set up by the Occupational Safety and Health Act (1970) to protect workers from hazardous conditions in the workplace.

**OSHA.** See **OCCUPATIONAL SAFETY AND HEALTH ADMINISTRATION.**

**RCRA.** See **RESOURCE CONSERVATION AND RECOVERY ACT.**

**RESOURCE CONSERVATION AND RECOVERY ACT (RCRA).** Established in 1976 as a regulatory system to track hazardous substances from creation to disposal. The agency requires safe procedures and prevents the careless or criminal dumping of hazardous substances. (3)

**SUPERFUND.** A sum of $1.6 billion, allocated under the Comprehensive Environment Response, Compensation, and Liability Act (1980), to cover the costs over five years of cleaning up hazardous substances, particularly in waste dump sites, which may endanger public health or welfare. About 86 percent comes from taxes on the manufacture or import of certain chemicals; the rest from general revenues. The original Superfund expired in September 1985, when Congress began deliberations on funding its extension.

**TOXIC SUBSTANCES CONTROL ACT (TSCA).** Passed in October 1976, the act gives the EPA ways to minimize dangers from toxic substances. It set up testing requirements, regulations, and means of keeping records. The act does not include pesticides, drugs, tobacco products, nuclear materials, cosmetics, foods, and food additives. Thus far, the TSCA has rarely been enforced.

**TOXIC SUBSTANCE STRATEGY COMMITTEE (TSSC).** Formed in 1977, the committee is a research team with members from eighteen federal agencies under the aegis of the President's Council on Environmental Quality. In 1980, the group reported the results of a three year study. They found that many Americans were killed each year by carcinogenic hazardous substances, and that deaths from cancer were increasing, even as other causes of death were declining.

**TSCA.** See **TOXIC SUBSTANCES CONTROL ACT.**

**TSSC.** See **TOXIC SUBSTANCES STRATEGY COMMITTEE.**

# THE SUBSTANCES

# A

**ACETALDEHYDE** ($C_2H_4O$; a colorless flammable liquid with a pungent, fruity odor; standard 200 ppm). Used in the manufacture of acetic acid, perfumes, aniline dyes, synthetic rubber, plastics, drugs, and for silvering mirrors. It is irritating to mucous membranes and dangerous to the eyes. Inhaling the substance depresses the central nervous system, and ingesting it produces symptoms of "drunkenness." Tiny amounts of the substance occur naturally in many fruits and berries. It is used in small quantities to give the flavor of butter, chocolate, banana, or peaches to beverages, ice cream, candy, and baked goods, among other foods.

**ACETONE** ($C_3H_6O$; a colorless flammable liquid solvent with a mintlike odor; standard 1,000 ppm). Used in the manufacture of airplane dopes, nail-polish remover, rayon, and photographic film. It is also found in the food industry for processing fats and oils. Continued use is irritating to the eyes and respiratory tract. In large amounts it causes headaches, faintness, and unconsciousness. Also called ketone propane and propanone.

**ACID RAIN.** Rainfall that contains particularly high amounts of sulfuric acid and nitric acid. It is caused by the emission of large amounts of sulfur dioxide and nitrogen oxides into the air, where they dissolve in rainwater to form dilute acid. The government estimates that about 22.5 million tons of sulfur dioxide and 15 million tons of nitrogen oxides are released into the air every year. The major sources are coal-burning power plants, metal-working factories, and automobiles.

The sulfur dioxide and nitrogen oxide particles are often carried long distances. As they combine with rainwater, they form the sulfuric and nitric acids. Areas suffering acid rain damage, therefore, may be very far from the place where the emissions originated.

Over the last 25 years raindrops have become some 50 times more acidic. The result is that fish and plants in lakes are being killed, forests are dying or growing more slowly, and food crops are yielding less per acre. The acid rain also eats away at stone buildings and automobile finishes. And it gets into the water supply, allowing the lead in water pipes to leach into the drinking water.

The National Academy of Sciences reports that as the emission of acid-causing fumes increases, the percentage of acid in rainwater goes up. According to the EPA, acid rain poses "little direct risk to human health." But the National Academy of Sciences considers it "a threat to human welfare because of its potential impact on materials, forest and farm productivity, aquatic ecosystems and drinking water systems."

Two main ways have been suggested for dealing with the problem of acid rain. The first requires that contributors to the acid rain problem adopt specific ways and means of reducing emissions, such as a scrubber (to remove sulfur oxides from flue gas), or "washing" coal before it is burned (to remove part of the sulfur). The second approach sets standards, but leaves it up to the sources to find their own ways of reducing emissions. To date, all proposals to deal with acid rain have been hindered by two difficulties: identifying the sources and agreeing on how to avoid the problem. (11)

**ACRYLONITRILE (AN)** ($C_3H_3N$; a clear colorless flammable liquid; standard 2 ppm). Used chiefly in the manufacture of synthetic rubber, fibers, and plastics. About 1.5 billion pounds are produced per year in the United States, and of this amount

2.6 million pounds are emitted from the 37 factories producing the chemical. Over 125,000 workers are exposed to acrylonitrile in the workplace. The chemical gives off poisonous vapors which can explode and, if burned, produces deadly cyanide gases. It can also be inhaled, swallowed, or cause damage by direct contact. Slight exposure can cause eye irritation, nausea, vomiting, headaches, and dizziness. Severe exposure causes profound weakness, convulsions, asphyxia, and death. Animal experiments show that exposure can lead to several types of cancers as well as genetic damage. Epidemiological studies indicate an increase in brain, lung, prostate, and colon cancers. Occasional deaths result from extreme exposure. Also called propene nitrile or vinyl cyanide. (30, 31)


**AGENT ORANGE.** An herbicide sprayed by the American army in Vietnam from 1965 to 1970 to remove forest cover and kill the crops of the enemy, the Viet Cong. The substance consisted of equal parts of the herbicides 2,4-D and 2,4,5-T (50 million pounds), along with a contaminant, dioxin (350 pounds). Agent Orange was very effective in removing some 70 percent of the ground cover. Soon, though, large numbers of birth defects were discovered among infants born to Vietnamese families that were exposed to Agent Orange. Later, American veterans who returned from Vietnam began reporting an unusually high incidence of cancer and children with birth defects.

Several studies done in the United States revealed no link between Agent Orange and these conditions. In September 1984, though, the U.S. government launched a ten-year investigation, called Agent Orange Project, to determine whether Agent Orange did indeed affect the health of the servicemen who handled the chemical. See also **2,4-DICHLOROPHENOXY-ACETIC ACID, DIOXIN,** and **2,4,5-TRICHLOROPHENOXY-ACETIC ACID.** (11)

**ALDRIN** ($C_{12}H_8Cl_6$; a colorless crystalline solid; standard 0.25 mg/m$^3$). Aldrin is a pesticide whose use was restricted by the government in 1974. Its effects on humans range from headaches, dizziness, nausea, and vomiting, to tremors, convulsions, and kidney damage. To get rid of stray dogs, aldrin-treated meat was put on the streets of Bahia, Brazil. Thirteen children ate the meat. They became violently ill, perspired profusely, vomited, foamed at the mouth, had convulsions, and died. Aldrin has also proven toxic to fish and birds. (11)

**ALKANES** (standard 1,000 ppm). A group of similar chemicals, sometimes called paraffins, that make up a major part of natural gas and petroleum. Their effects are seen mostly in the central nervous system and the skin. In low concentrations alkanes can cause anesthesia and loss of consciousness; at high concentrations they can cause cell damage and death. See also **ALKENES** and **AROMATICS**.

**ALKENES.** Formed in large quantities during the breaking down of the large molecules in crude oils. They are common in refined petroleum products such as gasoline. Alkenes are generally more toxic than alkanes but less toxic than aromatics. See also **ALKANES** and **AROMATICS**.

**ALLYL CHLORIDE** ($C_3H_5Cl$; a colorless flammable liquid with an unpleasant odor; standard 1 ppm). Used in the manufacture of glycerol and other chemical products. It is a strong poison and a dangerous fire hazard. The vapors are very irritating to the eyes, nose, and throat. Contact of the liquid with the skin may result in numbness and burns. Inhalation causes headaches, dizziness, and in high concentration, loss of consciousness. Repeated exposure is known to damage the respiratory tract, liver, and kidneys. Also called 3-chloropropene.

**ALLYL SULFIDE** ($C_6H_{10}S$; a colorless toxic liquid with a garlic odor; no federal standard). Used in dehydrating onions and as a fruit and garlic flavoring agent for beverages, ice cream, ices, baked goods, candy, and meats. It produces irritation of the eyes and respiratory tract among workers handling the substance. A high level of exposure can cause unconsciousness; long-term exposure can cause liver and kidney damage. Also called garlic oil.

**ALUMINUM** (Al; a metallic element). Used in alloys, and for making lightweight utensils, castings, airplane parts, and so on. It is found in nature in igneous rock, shale, clay, and most soils. Aluminum is toxic to animal and plant cells, and can damage the eyes, skin and upper respiratory tract if used improperly. No hazard has been detected in the use of aluminum cooking utensils, etc. Deaths have been reported in those workers in smelting and refining industries who inhale large quantities of very finely ground metallic aluminum, and among individuals exposed to aluminum oxide dust over a long period of time. The latter illness is known as "Shaver's disease." Aluminum is called aluminium in Canada.

**3-AMINO-1,2,4-TRIAZOLE** ($C_2H_4N_4$; a colorless crystalline solid). It is an herbicide that was developed in 1954 and was used primarily to kill weeds along railroad tracks and on croplands. In 1958 it was certified by the Agriculture Department for use on croplands only after the harvest. Just before Thanksgiving, 1959, heavy concentrations were found on the cranberry crop. The government ordered the destruction of several million pounds of cranberries because evidence showed that the chemical could cause cancer. All uses were banned in 1971. Currently, disposal is regulated as a hazardous waste product. The substance is being studied to see if regulation of noncropland use is necessary.

**AMMONIA** ($NH_3$; a colorless nonflammable gas with a sharp odor; standard 50 ppm). Used in the manufacture of fertilizers, dyes, synthetic fibers, and plastics, and as a refrigerant and household cleaner. Exposure affects the respiratory system and can be extremely irritating to mucous membranes, eyes, and skin. It can also cause headaches, salivation, throat burning, nausea, and vomiting.

**AMYL ALCOHOL** ($C_5H_{12}O$; a highly flammable liquid with a camphor odor; standard 100-200 ppm). The food industry uses amyl alcohol in low concentrations as a chocolate, apple, banana, and liquor flavoring agent. It is known to be irritating to the eyes and upper respiratory tract. Inhalation causes violent coughing. Ingestion of small quantities causes vertigo and headache; large amounts can be fatal.

**AN.** See **ACRYLONITRILE.**

**ANESTHETIC GASES.** Used to induce loss of sensation during medical or dental surgery. Exposure of doctors, dentists, nurses, and other operating room personnel to the gases can lead to miscarriages, birth defects, decreased alertness, and slowed reaction time. The substances may also cause some types of cancer.

**ANTHRACENE** ($C_{14}H_{10}$; yellow crystals with blue fluorescence; no federal standard). A part of petroleum that is used in the manufacture of dyes. The product causes skin damage and perhaps cancer of nasal cavity, larynx, lungs, skin, and scrotum. See also **AROMATICS.**

**ANTIMONY** (Sb; a metallic element; standard 0.5 mg/m$^3$). Used in the rubber, printing, and pigment industries. The element occurs in nature, either free or combined with other elements. Most exposure of this toxic material occurs during mining and smelting operations. Antimony can irritate the skin, eyes, nose, and throat. Severe exposure can damage the heart, lungs, respiratory tract, and may lead to coma and death; it is also believed to be carcinogenic.

**AQUA FORTIS.** See **NITRIC ACID.**

**AROMATICS.** A group of hydrocarbons that have an agreeable odor. They include anthracene, benzene, and naphthalene. Aromatics are considered to be the most toxic hydrocarbons found in petroleum, and are present in all crude oils and many petroleum products. Many aromatics are soluble in water to some extent. This increases their danger to organisms that live in lakes, rivers, and oceans. Certain aromatics are considered long-term poisons and are suspected to be carcinogens. See also **ANTHRACENE, BENZENE,** and **NAPHTHALENE.**

**ARSENIC** (As; a grayish-white element; standard 0.001 mg/m$^3$). A poison, it is used mostly in pesticides and herbicides. Even though it occurs naturally in the soil, it is also a by-product of copper and lead smelting. Exposed workers in copper, zinc, and lead smelting industries are, therefore, those mostly affected. A 1969 study showed three times the rate of lung and liver cancer among arsenic-exposed smelters. Chronic inhalation causes weakness, loss of appetite, nausea, and diarrhea. Severe exposure is linked to lung, liver, and skin cancer. Consumers may be exposed to arsenic through contaminated drinking water, lumber products impregnated with preservatives, and air emissions from smelting, pesticide, and glass manufacturing plants. Between 1975 and 1980 the federal government set limits on the air emission of arsenic and on the amounts permissible in drinking water. It also regulated the disposal of this material. (43)

**ARSENICALS.** See **WOOD PRESERVATIVES.**

**ARSENIC HYDRIDE. See ARSINE.**

**ARSINE** ($AsH_3$; a colorless flammable gas with a bad, garlic-like odor; standard 0.05 ppm). The substance is used to place circuits on computer chips. It is sometimes released accidentally from unusual places. For example, someone cleaning out steel tanks that contained concentrated sulfuric acid was exposed to arsine. It is fatal in large quantities. A man who inhaled the gas by mistake in June 1984 was hopitalized shortly afterwards with kidney failure; he died 11 days later. Small amounts cause skin and lung cancer, mood swings, and paranoia. Also called arsenic hydride.

**ASBESTOS** (a white chalky mineral; standard 2 asbestos fibers per cubic centimeter of air). A general term for various fibrous minerals; the most widely used are chrysotile (white asbestos, the most common), crocidolite (blue asbestos), amosite (brown asbestos), anthophyllite, and tremolite. It is found in thousands of construction products, including flooring, roofing, insulation, wallboard, and piping as well as in automobile and truck brake linings, paints, patching compounds, and various fireproof fabrics and materials. Asbestos is used for its ability to resist heat, salt water, and corrosive chemicals, and for its insulating qualities. Since World War II about 800,000 tons of asbestos have been used yearly, about two-thirds going into the construction of homes, factories, schools, ships, and other types of buildings and structures.

The government estimates that about 50,000 workers are involved in the manufacture of asbestos, with another 2,500,000 handling products containing asbestos. In the 40 to 50 years asbestos has been in use, about 11 million workers and their families have been exposed to this substance. According to the EPA, 15 million students are potentially threatened by dust from flaking asbestos in 14,000 of the nation's 36,000 schools. A 1984 survey showed that 700,000 other public buildings—federal buildings, office buildings, and apartment houses—contain asbestos that is crumbling. Further, as many as 200,000 private homes have high levels of asbestos in their forced air heating systems. In fact, that same EPA survey found that 42 of the EPA's 270 buildings had loose asbestos! It is believed that there is a total of about 30 million tons of asbestos in the nation's buildings, and that it will cost up to $3 billion to clean it up.

When inhaled, asbestos fibers can cause two diseases: asbestosis and cancer. Asbestosis is a permanent, progressive disease that cannot be cured. The symptoms are shortness of breath, pain in the upper chest or back, and a dry sound, called rales, during breathing. As a result of the difficulty in breathing the victim's fingers and toes become "clubbed," that is, rounded with flattened nails. Asbestos seems implicated in a number of different types of cancer, including that of the lung, the larynx, and the digestive tract, as well as pleural mesothelioma (cancer of the lining of the lungs), and peritoneal mesothelioma (cancer of the lining of the abdominal cavity), both of which are rare in the general population, but common among asbestos workers.

Studies show that about 7 percent of asbestos workers die of asbestosis, 20 percent die of lung cancer, 9 percent die of pleural and peritoneal mesotheliomas, and 4 percent die of cancer somewhere in the digestive system. Any asbestos worker who smokes is 90 times more likely to develop lung cancer than a nonsmoker. According to Dr. Irving J. Selikoff, Director of the Mount Sinai Medical Center Environmental Sciences Laboratory, every hour of the day and night someone dies from asbestos exposure, and there have been some 350,000 unnecessary deaths in the United States because of asbestos. It has actually caused more cancer deaths than any other known carcinogen, except tobacco.

Since the 1970s, the government has been gradually restricting the use of asbestos: In 1972 its use was banned in clothing; 1973 saw an end to spraying it on buildings for fireproofing; in 1976 OSHA limited the allowed exposure of workers to 2 asbestos fibers per cubic centimeter of air; in 1977 a law was passed forbidding its use in patching compounds and in gas heaters; in 1979 manufacturers voluntarily agreed to stop placing it in hair dyers; in 1986 the EPA proposed a ten-year program to ban the use of all products containing asbestos. See also **INDOOR POLLUTION.** (17, 32)


**ASPARTAME.** A synthetic sweetener that is some 200 times as sweet as sugar. It is made up of two amino acids, phenylalanine and aspartic acid. Aspartame is sold under the trade name of NutraSweet in diet soft drinks, and Equal as a powdered sweetener. Although previous tests showed aspartame to be safe, in 1984 the Centers for Disease Control did a study of 592 complaints of headaches, digestive disorders, and rashes believed to be connected with the artificial sweetener. The finding, announced on November 1, 1984, was that there is no "evidence of serious, widespread, adverse health consequences." Early in 1985, though, Dr. Richard Wurtman of the Massachusetts Institute of Technology said some consumers were taking in aspartame at levels that have been linked to bad effects on brain chemicals in animal studies.

**AURAMINE** (a yellow crystalline solid). Used chiefly as a dye for paper, leather, and other products. Mostly rubber workers, textile dyers, paint and dye manufacturers are affected. The substance produces bladder cancer.

**AZOTIC ACID.** See **NITRIC ACID.**

# B

**BACTERIAL POLLUTION**. Disease-causing bacteria that are found in household and municipal waste. Exposure to these bacteria can lead to serious illness and disease, and in extreme cases, to death. Although there has been much progress in recent decades in controlling bacterial pollution, it still remains a significant problem.

**BCME**. See **BIS(CHLOROMETHYL) ETHER**.

**BENOMYL** ($C_{14}H_{18}N_4O_3$; a colorless crystalline solid). Used as a pesticide and fungicide. The material has a low toxicity, but in 1984 the EPA agreed to conduct further investigations of possible dangers.

**BENZALDEHYDE** ($C_7H_6O$; a flammable liquid). Used in small quantities to add flavor to beverages, ice cream, ices, candy, baked goods, chewing gum, and cordials. It is known to cause allergic symptoms as well as central nervous system depression and convulsions when taken in large amounts. If ingested, a fatal dose is about two ounces. Also called benzoic aldehyde.

**BENZENE** ($C_6H_6$; a clear colorless flammable liquid with a strong pleasant odor; standard 1 ppm). The compound is obtained from coal tar and most of it (86 percent of the amount produced) is used in the manufacture of organic chemicals. The rest is used as an octane booster additive in gasoline and to produce detergents, pesticides, solvents, and paint removers. Over 14 billion pounds are produced in the United States each year, making it the third most widely used chemical.

Benzene has long been known to affect the blood, causing severe anemia, bone marrow damage, and leukemia. Studies from 1974 through 1977 linked benzene exposure directly to increased leukemia among the 3 million refinery and coke-oven workers, and others who handle this dangerous substance. A more recent study shows a two- to eight-fold increase in leukemia deaths among workers exposed for ten years at the current permissible level. According to the NTP, if 10,000 people are exposed to a level of only 1 ppm for one year, one to four will develop leukemia. If the period of exposure is extended to 30 years, as many as 110 may fall ill with the same disease. Besides the workers, the EPA estimates that three-quarters of the population is exposed to detectable levels of benzene through the air and water. The material is also toxic to some fish and other sea creatures.

The results of benzene inhalation can be acute or chronic, depending on the length and concentration of the exposure. Acute poisoning occurs in a matter of minutes. The effects are depression of the central nervous system, headache, dizziness, nausea, convulsions, coma, and finally death. In cases of mild chronic poisoning, the victim suffers irritation of the skin and becomes confused and hysterical, laughs, shouts, curses, sings, and becomes very stubborn. The persisting symptoms are breathlessness, nervous irritability, and unsteady gait. In severe instances, the person can develop aplastic anemia or leukemia.

In 1977 OSHA ordered a 90 percent reduction in the maximum level of benzene permitted in factories, from 10 ppm to 1 ppm. In 1980, however, the Supreme Court rejected the lower limit and restored the previous limit of 10 ppm. Other regulations in 1980 limited water contamination and waste disposal, and required the prompt reporting of spills from benzene. Also called benzol. See also **AROMATICS.**

**BENZIDINE** ($C_{12}H_{12}N_2$ ; a crystalline solid; no federal standard). Used chiefly in dye manufacture, especially azo dyes, such as Congo Red. In the body it is transformed into a carcinogen that is believed to cause bladder and pancreatic cancer. NIOSH recommends stringent work practices and controls as well as replacement with less toxic materials where possible.

**BENZOIC ALDEHYDE.** See **BENZALDEHYDE.**

**BENZOL.** See **BENZENE.**

**BENZYL ACETATE** ($C_9H_{10}O_2$ ; a colorless flammable liquid with a floral odor). Used as a synthetic raspberry, strawberry, cherry, banana, and plum flavoring agent for beverages, ice cream, ices, candy, baked goods, chewing gum, and gelatin desserts. If ingested in excess amounts, it can cause gastrointestinal irritation, vomiting, and diarrhea. Contact can be irritating to the skin, eyes, and respiratory tract.

**BENZYL ALCOHOL** ($C_7H_8O$; a flammable white liquid with a faint sweet odor; no federal standard). Used as a solvent in perfumes, as a local anesthetic, and as a synthetic fruit flavoring for beverages, ice cream, ices, candy, baked goods, gelatin desserts, and chewing gum. Poisoned mice suffer respiratory and muscular paralysis, convulsions, and narcosis. In large amounts humans find it irritating and corrosive to the skin and mucous membranes. Ingestion can cause vomiting, diarrhea, and depression of the central nervous system. Also called hydroxytoluene.

**BERYLLIUM** (Be; a very light, steel-gray metallic element; standard 0.002 mg/m$^3$). Used in nuclear reactors, autos, computers, business machines, aerospace products, and electronics. The material is also widely used in industry as an alloy material for copper and steel. It has been used for making cathode tubes for television and for fluorescent tubes, as well as in the ceramics and allied industries.

Beryllium can be hazardous to humans working with the substance, their families, and even to persons using the laundries where their work clothes are washed. Just a few minutes of exposure to a high level of beryllium can cause beryllium poisoning, affecting the skin, eyes, and respiratory system. About 12 new cases of beryllium poisoning are reported in the United States every year. More frequent are effects from inhaling the fumes or dust of beryllium, which leads to inflammation of the throat and nose membranes, and to pneumonia-like symptoms—coughing, difficulty in breathing, pain and tightness in the chest, loss of appetite and weight loss, and a general weakness and tiredness. The mild cases can recover in one to six weeks. The more severe cases take six months or longer. Sometimes a chronic condition permanently affects the lungs, kidneys, liver, or bones. There is also some evidence that it is a carcinogen, producing cancers of the liver, gall bladder, and bile ducts.

One of the greatest difficulties in diagnosing diseases associated with beryllium is the long latency period. The symptoms may develop three months to nine years after exposure. The prognosis in advanced cases is very poor, and mortality is high. (34)

**BHOPAL, INDIA, CHEMICALS.** The city in central India where a gas leak killed about 2,000 and injured as many as 200,000 on December 3, 1984. It is considered the worst hazardous substance accident in history.

The tragedy occurred when the deadly gas, methyl isocyanate (MIC), leaked from a Union Carbide factory in Bhopal, a city of about one million inhabitants. Methyl isocyanate is used to make the pesticide Sevin Carbaryl. This pesticide works against some 180 types of insects and is used to protect as many as 100 different crops. The MIC at Bhopal was stored in three partly buried tanks within the plant. Each tank held 40 tons of the deadly chemical.

The experts are still not sure what caused the gas leak. It could have been a sharp change in temperature. Perhaps some impurities had gotten into the tank. There might have been a tiny crack in a tank wall. In any case, the pressure and the temperature in the tank began to rise, inching higher and higher. The gas started seeping out.

Even at this stage, though, there should have been no real danger. There was a "scrubber" system that was designed to make the gas harmless. But for some reason, the scrubber did not work.

The MIC was already leaking as a white cloud over the plant when a night-shift worker noticed that the pressure in the tank was above the danger level. He called a supervisor, who rushed over to the plant. In 30 minutes the tank was sealed. But in those 30 minutes at least five tons of MIC escaped into the air.

Gradually the winds carried the poison vapors over Bhopal. By now it was two o'clock in the morning. Most of Bhopal was asleep when the factory siren went off. Many residents, thinking it was a fire, awoke and rushed toward the plant. They ran right into the path of the burning, choking gas. One man said, "It was like breathing fire."

Coughing and screaming, the people surged through the streets. The young and healthy were vomiting and shrieking that they were going blind. The old and sickly were collapsing on the ground and dying.

By dawn, Bhopal looked as though a neutron bomb had exploded over the city. The streets were littered with the sick and the dead. But the buildings were unharmed. For days the city was in chaos. The hospitals and cemeteries could not begin to keep up with the need. Doctors and rescue workers from other cities worked to help the hapless victims of the disaster. But they had little success. The death toll kept rising. After a week or two, though, the MIC was gone. Just the survivors were left; many permanently blind, sterile, brain damaged, and with liver and kidney disease. See also **METHYL ISOCYANATE.**

**4-BIPHENYLAMINE** ($C_{12}H_{11}N$; a yellowish-brown crystalline solid). Once used in the manufacture of synthetic rubber, it is now banned. The material caused bladder cancer in chemical workers, usually after a latency period as long as 30 years.

**BIS(CHLOROMETHYL) ETHER (BCME)** ($C_2H_4Cl_2O$; a colorless liquid with a suffocating odor; standard 0.001 ppm). Used in the manufacture of polymers. BCME causes skin and eye damage and is believed to cause lung cancer. Mostly affected are chemical workers involved in producing certain resins.

**BLUE 1, BLUE 2.** See **FOOD COLORS.**

**BROMOMETHANE.** See **METHYL BROMIDE.**

**1,3-BUTADIENE** ($C_4H_6$; a colorless gas; standard 1,000 ppm). A chemical widely used in the manufacture of synthetic rubber and plastic products. In 1983, 2.3 billion pounds of 1,3-butadiene were produced in the United States. In February 1985 researchers at the National Institute of Environmental

Health Sciences reported that 1,3-butadiene could cause cancer in mice at exposure levels much lower than the government standard. The mice developed cancer of the heart, lungs, spleen, liver, kidneys, and stomach. In fact, the study was stopped after 61 weeks instead of going for the planned 103 weeks because so few of the mice were still alive. In October 1985 the EPA reported that 1,3-butadiene was causing up to 23 cancer deaths per year among exposed workers, and that they planned to ban it as a hazardous carcinogen.

**BUTANONE.** See **METHYL ETHYL KETONE.**

**BUTYL ACETATE** ($C_6H_{12}O_2$; a colorless flammable liquid; standard 150 ppm). Used in lacquer thinners and solvents, and also as a synthetic flavoring agent in foods. In humans, the substance may cause pinkeye and other eye irritations. High doses depress the central nervous system and produce narcotic effects.

**BUTYL ALCOHOL** ($C_4H_{10}O$; a colorless flammable liquid with a disagreeable odor; standard 100 ppm). Used as a solvent for waxes, fats, resins, and shellac. It is also a synthetic flavoring agent for beverages, ice cream, ices, candy, baked goods, cordials, and cream. The substance is known to irritate mucous membranes and can cause dermatitis, headache, dizziness, and drowsiness. In severe cases, liver damage may result.

**BUTYL BUTYRATE** ($C_8H_{16}O_2$; a water-white toxic liquid with an applelike odor; standard 400 ppm). Used in flavoring beverages, ice cream, ices, candy, and baked goods to give a taste of butter, apple, banana, peach, or nut. In high concentrations it may have irritating and narcotic effects.

# C

**CADMIUM** (Cd; silver-white metallic element; 0.1 mg/m³). One of the most highly toxic metals, cadmium is mostly used in metal plating and in making certain alloys. It causes injury through inhalation of its fumes or ingestion of its soluble salts. This is a hazard in the smelting of cadmium ores, working with residues, production of cadmium compounds, spraying of cadmium-bearing paints and pigments, welding of alloys containing cadmium, cadmium plating processes, and melting of the metal itself. Another danger is in eating or drinking acidic foods and beverages that have been standing in cadmium-plated containers. In addition, cadmium enters the soil water and drinking water supply, is found in acid rain, and is toxic to fish.

Once in the body it is a cumulative poison, and the cadmium stays in the liver and kidneys. The effects of mild cadmium poisoning are coughing, sweating, and chest pain. In the more acute form, there is lung damage, possible damage to the kidneys and bones, and changes in the blood. The first symptoms are diarrhea, nausea, and abdominal pain. One very noticeable symptom of cadmium poisoning is a yellow ring that forms around the gums at the tooth line. Cadmium poisoning is a suspected cause of lung and prostate cancer, and possibly leads to birth defects.

**CAFFEINE** ($C_8 H_{10} N_4 O_2$; an odorless white powder). A natural part of coffee and tea, it is used as an additive to give "kick" to soft drinks. A cup of coffee usually contains about 125 mg, tea has 60 mg, cocoa has 50 mg, and cola drinks have between 40 and 72 mg per serving. Caffeine acts as a stimulant on the central nervous system, heart, and respiratory systems. It can cause nervousness, insomnia, irregular heartbeat, noise in the ears, and in high enough doses, convulsions. The substance is known to alter blood sugar release and its uptake by the liver. Its safety as an additive and its potential to cause birth defects are under study.

**CALCIUM CHLORIDE** ($CaCl_2$; colorless crystals). Used to preserve wood and fireproof materials, in automobile and highway de-icing, and as a dust control on unpaved roads. In the food industry it is used as a firming agent for sliced apples and other fruits, as a jelly ingredient, and in canned tomatoes. If this material comes in contact with the eyes, it causes irritation. Ingestion may cause stomach upset and heart irregulartities.

**CALCIUM HYPOCHLORITE** ($Ca\ Cl_2\ O_2$; a white powder with a strong chlorine odor). Used as a germicide and a sterilizing agent. It is the active ingredient of chlorinated lime, used in the processing of cottage cheese and in sugar refining. The substance is used to sterilize fruit and vegetables in a 50 percent solution. Dilute calcium hypochlorite is also found in laundry bleach and household bleach. It is very irritating to the eyes, skin, and mucous membranes. Ingestion may cause pain and inflammation of the mouth, pharynx, esophagus, and stomach.

**CALCIUM OXIDE** ($CaO$; colorless crystals or white powder; standard 5 $mg/m^3$). Used as a component in the manufacture of bricks, plaster, mortar, stucco, fungicides, and insecticides. In the food industry it is a yeast food and dough conditioner for bread, rolls, and buns, a clarifier for beet- and cane-sugar juices, and an alkali for dairy products, such as ice cream. A strong caustic, in high concentrations calcium oxide can cause dermatitis and can severely irritate eyes, mucous membranes, and the upper respiratory tract. Also called quicklime.

**CAMPHOR** ($C_{10}H_{16}O$; white transparent crystals with a pungent odor; standard 2 mg/m$^3$). Used as a moth repellent, in embalming fluid, as a preservative in cosmetics, in the manufacture of explosives, in lacquers, and in liniments and topical anesthetics. It is also found in spice flavorings for beverages, baked goods, and condiments. Camphor is readily absorbed into the body, causing blurred vision, mental confusion, delirium, coma, respiratory failure, and death. Ingestion by a pregnant woman can cause the death of the fetus.

**CARBARYL** ($C_{12}H_{11}NO_2$; white powder; standard 5 mg/m$^3$). Used mostly as an insecticide. In humans it affects the nervous system, causing nausea and vomiting, cramps, dimness of vision, dizziness, headaches, difficulty in breathing, and general weakness. There is evidence that carbaryl causes birth defects, alters genes, and is carcinogenic as well.

**CARBON BICHLORIDE** ($C_2Cl_4$; a clear colorless liquid; standard 100 ppm). Biggest use is in dry cleaning; also used as a degreasing agent, a fumigant, and to remove intestinal worms in animals. In addition to dermatitis and eye and nose irritations, this substance has a passing narcotic effect on the victim. The toxin is very damaging to the liver, heart, and kidney, and when it attacks the central nervous system, leads to death. Also known as carbon dichloride or ethylene tetrachloride.

**CARBOLIC ACID.** See **PHENOL.**

**CARBON BISULFIDE.** See **CARBON DISULFIDE.**

**CARBON DICHLORIDE.** See **CARBON BICHLORIDE.**

**CARBON DISULFIDE** ($CS_2$; a flammable liquid; standard 20 ppm). Widely used in the manufacture of cellophane, rayon, and textiles, and as a solvent in the rubber industry. It is also used as a fumigant in grain elevators. Inhalation of the vapor or prolonged or repeated contact with the skin can affect the heart, damage the central nervous system, lead to psychological disturbances, and produce changes in both the male and female reproductive systems. Symptoms are nervousness, indigestion, irritability, insomnia, excessive fatigue, loss of appetite, and headache. Further signs of poisoning are a waxy pallor, low blood pressure, tremors, and unusual behavior. The EPA banned the use of carbon disulfide as a fumigant on December 31, 1985. Also called carbon bisulfide.

**CARBON MONOXIDE** (CO; a colorless odorless flammable highly poisonous gas; standard 50 ppm). A major air pollutant, carbon monoxide is produced when fuels containing carbon are burned without sufficient air. A major source is the exhaust of gasoline-burning vehicles. It also comes from electric furnaces, blast furnaces, gas manufacturing plants, oil distilleries, charcoal ovens, refuse plants, kilns, and coal mines. Kerosene heaters and charcoal grills produce carbon monoxide, and it sometimes seeps into houses from attached garages.

Carbon monoxide is picked up by blood cells in the body about ten times as fast as oxygen, thereby depriving the body of the oxygen it needs. Broadly speaking, anyone who is in an area where a fuel is being burned may fall victim to carbon monoxide poisoning. Drivers of cars, trucks, or buses, garage mechanics, and tunnel and toll booth attendants, for example, can be overcome by carbon monoxide gas, which they cannot even smell.

Among the symptoms of mild poisoning are nausea, dizziness, and headaches; symptoms of severe poisoning are brain or heart damage, collapse, and death in minutes by suffocation. It is also a safety hazard, since the drowsiness, poor coordination, and confusion that it causes can result in accidents. About 2,000 Americans die each year from carbon monoxide poisoning; 10,000 more suffer harmful effects.

**CARBON OXYCHLORIDE.** See **PHOSGENE.**

**CARBON TETRACHLORIDE** ($CCl_4$ ; a colorless nonflammable liquid; standard 10 ppm). Used in fumigants and pesticides, as a solvent, a refrigerant, cleaning fluid, and to remove grease and oil from machinery and other apparatus. Carbon tetrachloride is immediately dangerous to the eyes, skin, and mucous membranes. When small amounts are consumed regularly over long periods, such as in pesticide residues on grain, it may severely damage liver and kidney function, depress the central nervous system, and cause various digestive-system symptoms. There is a risk of liver cancer as well. The EPA banned the use of carbon tetrachloride as a fumigant on December 31, 1985. Also called perchloromethane.

**CARBONYL CHLORIDE.** See **PHOSGENE.**

**CAUSTIC POTASH.** See **POTASSIUM HYDROXIDE.**

**CFCS.** See **CHLOROFLUOROCARBONS.**

**CHAMOMILE.** The most popular tea in the world is made from this flowering plant. Over 1 million cups are drunk daily. It can, though, cause an allergic reaction in some people, resulting in runny nose, watery eyes, and sneezing.

**CHERNOBYL RADIATION.** At 1:23 A.M. on April 26, 1986, the worst nuclear disaster to date took place at the Chernobyl nuclear power plant in the Ukraine region of the Soviet Union. It is believed that a blockage of the cooling tubes allowed the temperature in the core's uranium fuel to reach over 5000°F, causing an explosion that blew the roof off the reactor. Graphite, which was used to control the nuclear reaction in the core, ignited. A huge cloud of radioactive gas and particles escaped into the atmosphere and was carried around the world by the wind.

Two plant workers were killed, one by hot-steam burns, the other by falling debris. In addition, over 200 persons were hospitalized with radiation sickness, many of them in serious condition. Several subsequently died. The following day, the government evacuated over 90,000 people from the surrounding area and from Kiev.

There was serious danger of a meltdown, in which the molten uranium would work its way down through the earth to the water table below, making a nearby large water supply radioactive and spreading massive radiation throughout a large area. To control the radiation and put out the fire, helicopters dropped tons of sand, boron, clay, dolomite, and lead onto the reactor. Workers struggled to prevent a meltdown by encasing the reactor in concrete, including a thick layer under the reactor. While these measures were successful, experts believe that the radiation that had already escaped will lead to increased deaths from radiation sickness and cancer, and to birth defects in children born to those who had been exposed. The reactor will have to remain encased in concrete for hundreds of years.

**CHEWING TOBACCO.** See **SMOKELESS TOBACCO.**

**CHINONE.** See **QUINONE.**

**CHLORDANE** ($C_{10}H_6Cl_8$; a pale-yellow flammable liquid; standard 0.5 mg/m$^3$). An insecticide that is slightly more toxic than DDT. In large doses, chlordane causes cancer in animals, and is possibly just as dangerous in humans, though evidence is not clear. In small doses, however, it is known to affect respiration, digestion, and the central nervous system. The symptoms are blurred vision, confusion, delirium, coughing, abdominal pain, nausea, and vomiting, as well as convulsions. A veterinarian from Michigan who handled scout dogs in Vietnam and rubbed chlordane on the animals to kill their ticks and fleas, became paralyzed and blind. Many of the dogs also died of internal hemorrhaging. Since 1980 the substance has been largely banned. (11)

**CHLORINATED CAMPHENE.** See **TOXAPHENE.**

**CHLORINATED HYDROCARBONS.** A group of about 100 insecticides that persist in the environment and accumulate in the food chain. They also build up in human fat cells. The best known examples of chlorinated hydrocarbons are aldrin, benzenehexachloride, chlordane, DDT, dieldrin, endrin, heptachlor, hexachloride, kepone, PCBs, and toxaphene. Most have been banned or restricted because they cause birth defects, neurological disorder, and cancer and are harmful to wildlife. (8, 11)

**CHLORINATED NAPHTHALENES** (standard 0.5 mg/m$^3$). Used in the manufacture of cables, condensers, wires, storage batteries, and computer circuit boards. Typical symptoms of exposure include skin eruptions, headaches, fatigue, and loss of appetite. There are also internal injuries caused by these compounds; they mainly affect the liver.

**CHLOROETHYLENE.** See **VINYL CHLORIDE.**

**CHLOROFLUOROCARBONS** **(CFCs).** Man-made chemicals that served as the propellant in most aerosol products until this use was banned by the EPA and the FDA in 1977. They are still used, however, in aerosols in many other countries. And in the United States they are still employed as industrial solvents, as the coolant (called Freon) in refrigerators and air conditioners, for insulation, and for many other purposes. If no controls are imposed, the U.S. production of CFCs is expected to grow 7 percent a year; worldwide emissions are expected to increase 9 percent a year.

The large-scale release of CFCs into the atmosphere is believed to be destroying the ozone layer, which protects us from ultraviolet radiation from the sun and space. As the amount of ozone decreases, the danger of skin cancer from ultraviolet radiation increases. CFCs may also contribute to the so-called greenhouse effect—an inability of heat to escape from the earth's surface, contributing to a general warming of the global atmosphere.

The EPA has not yet regulated all uses of the CFCs. The reasons given include scientific uncertainty about their impact and the need to attack the problem worldwide. But recently other countries have begun to cut back production, and some are considering a limit on the use of CFCs in certain industries. Also known as fluorocarbons.

**CHLOROFORM** ($CHCl_3$; a clear colorless nonflammable pungent liquid; standard 50 ppm). Once widely used as an anesthetic, chloroform is no longer used for this purpose because of its toxic effects. About 160,000 tons, though, are now being produced annually, mostly to make fluorocarbon 22, a refrigerant. In 1977 the National Academy of Sciences said that chloroform causes liver or kidney disorders, birth defects, and central nervous system damage in experimental animals. Humans who are accidentally exposed to chloroform vapor may suffer damage to the heart or liver, which can prove fatal. Chloroform vapor enters the air when chlorine is added to water in water treatment plants. In 1976 and 1977 the National Cancer Institute found that high levels of chloroform cause cancer in rats and mice. The EPA, in September 1985, announced studies that showed that ingestion of chloroform could cause cancer in humans. As a result, the agency listed chloroform as a hazardous substance. Also called THM.

**CHLOROMETHANE. See METHYL CHLORIDE.**

**CHLOROMETHYL METHYL ETHER (CMME)** ($C_2H_4Cl_2O$; a flammable liquid). The vapors are very irritating. Used in plastic manufacturing plants, it affects chemical workers and may cause lung cancer.

**CHLOROPRENE** ($C_4H_5Cl$; a colorless flammable liquid; standard 25 ppm). Used in the production of artificial rubber. It may cause toxic symptoms upon inhalation. Small amounts can cause depression of the central nervous system and irreparable damage to vital organs, which may be severe enough to be fatal. Exposed workers often suffer hair loss and bad skin reactions.

**3-CHLOROPROPENE. See ALLYL CHLORIDE.**

**CHOLINESTERASE-INHIBITING PESTICIDES.** A group of pesticides that include carbaryl, ethion, fenthion, malathion, methomyl, and parathion.

**CHROMIUM** (Cr; a hard metallic element; standard 1 $mg/m^3$). Used mostly in alloys, such as stainless steel, and to plate other metals for hardness and corrosion resistance. It is also used in welding and in the manufacture of batteries, glass, pottery, and linoleum. An estimated 350,000 workers are at risk from this material. Chromium and its compounds can cause serious kidney and gastrointestinal damage, as well as irritation of the lung, nose, and skin. Workers who have been exposed to chromium show an increase in cancer of the lung, nasal cavity, sinuses, and the larynx, usually after a latency period of around 20 years. The substance is also toxic to some sea life.

**CMME.** See **CHLOROMETHYL METHYL ETHER.**

**COAL DUST** (standard 1.5 million particles/m$^3$). Miners, gashouse workers, stokers, and other coal producers suffer the effects of inhaling dust from anthracite and other kinds of coals. "Black lung disease" and "miner's asthma" are chronic diseases that are due to breathing air containing coal dust. They are characterized by shortness of breath, coughing, and chest pains in the early stages, with a general weakness and damage to the lungs and heart developing later.

**COAL TAR** (standard 0.2 mg/m$^3$). A black sticky residue left after soft coal has been distilled to make coal gas. The material affects those who work with coal tar or asphalt, coke-oven workers, miners, and chimney sweeps. Coal tar causes eye damage and is linked to cancer of the skin, lung, larynx, scrotum, and bladder.

**COBALT** (Co; a silver-white metallic element; standard 0.1 mg/m$^3$). Used in the manufacture of extremely hard steel and industrial tools. Powdered cobalt is mixed and hardened before being sawed, drilled, or ground into shape. If particles are inhaled, they can cause scarring of lung tissue. Symptoms of the asthma-like "hard-metals disease" include fatigue, shortness of breath, and sometimes emphysema. The disease may affect the heart, kidneys, and liver. It is permanent and progressive; there is no known cure.

**COKE-OVEN FUMES** (standard 0.15 mg/m$^3$). Hazardous emissions produced by heating coal in the absence of air to manufacture coke. About 61 million tons of coke are made in the United States every year. Coke is produced in massive ovens for use in steel-making blast furnaces and to extract metals from their ores, especially iron. Emissions from the coke ovens include solid particles, benzene, and traces of arsenic and cadmium. Coke-oven workers are at risk for genetic damage, bronchitis, and emphysema as well as lung, prostate, and kidney cancer. The NTP said the evidence of cancer is "overwhelming" based on both epidemiological and animal studies. In 1971 deaths among coke-oven workers from respiratory cancer was two times that of steel workers. Further, the NTP says that the "entire population is exposed at some level." At present there are no EPA controls on coke-oven emissions.(38)

**COMFREY.** An herb that promotes cell growth and, therefore, has long been used as a folk remedy for boils, bruises, and other types of skin wounds. Now, though, some people have taken to drinking a tea brewed from its leaves and roots. This is dangerous, since allantoin, a major ingredient of comfrey, has been found to be carcinogenic when ingested by rats. Comfrey also contains certain chemicals (pyrrolizidine alkaloids) that cause liver tumors in laboratory animals.

**COPPER** (Cu; a reddish-brown metallic element; standard 0.2 mg/m$^3$). Used as a conductor of heat and electricity and in the manufacture of alloys, such as brass and bronze. Copper compounds can cause eye damage and affect the liver and gastrointestinal tract. It is also toxic to young fish.

**COTTON DUST** (standard 0.2 mg/m$^3$). The fine powder that results from processing raw cotton. Inhaling cotton dust can cause a condition of the lungs known as byssinosis, or "brown lung disease." The symptoms include tightness of the chest and shortness of breath. It is especially noticeable to workers in cotton processing plants when they return to work after several days off. This had led to the nickname, "Monday fever." If detected early enough, "brown lung disease" is reversible. But long-term exposure often results in a condition that is permanent, crippling, and eventually fatal. An estimated 35,000 cotton workers are already crippled by "brown lung disease." (40)

**CREOSOTE** (Yellowish to dark green-brown flammable oily liquid with a penetrating odor; standard 0.1 mg/m$^3$). Creosote is a poisonous material that is used as a preservative. It is obtained from coal tar or wood tar. Workers who are exposed to this material may suffer skin irritations. After an incubation period of 12 to 30 years, there is also the possibility of cancer of the lung, skin, larynx, or nasal cavity. See also **COAL TAR.**

**CRISTABOLITE.** See **SILICA.**

**CYANIDES.** Any of a large group of salts, such as the highly poisonous potassium cyanide (KCN) and sodium cyanide (NaCN). Poisoning by cyanides may occur by absorption through the skin, through ingestion, or by inhalation. Workers exposed daily to these materials, in electroplating and pickling industries, for example, may develop an itchy skin condition known as "cyanide rash." In high concentrations, giddiness, headache, unconsciousness, and convulsions may appear. Lower concentrations may cause irritations of the throat, difficulty in breathing, headache, and weakness. It is toxic to fish, killing some, reducing the growth and development in others.

**CYCLAMATES.** Nonsugar, low-calorie sweeteners, about 30 times as sweet as refined sugar. Big use of cyclamates started in the 1960s at a time when diet foods were becoming very popular. The National Academy of Sciences warned in 1962 and 1968 that the public should not use artificial sweeteners. In 1969 the FDA found that cyclamates cause bladder cancer, birth defects, and mutations in animals. At that time, an estimated 175 million Americans were ingesting large amounts of cyclamates in many products from chewing gum to soft drinks. Because of a long latency period, much is yet unknown about the cancer dangers to humans. In April 1969 the FDA recommended that people restrict their intake of cyclamates. In October 1969 they banned the substances completely, ordering them off the shelves by February 1970. That same month, under industrial pressure, the FDA reversed itself, approving cyclamates if labeled "drugs." But finally, in August 1970, they were banned again.

**CYCLOHEXANE** ($C_6H_{12}$; a colorless flammable liquid with a pungent odor; standard 300 ppm). Used industrially as a substitute for benzene and toluene, and in foods as an artificial butter- and fruit-flavoring agent for beverages, ice cream, ices, candy, and baked goods. In acute poisoning, the symptoms consist of disturbances in equilibrium, giddiness, and stupor, followed by paralysis of the respiratory center. Although the effects are usually temporary, in high concentrations it can also cause narcosis and possible liver and kidney damage.

**CYMEN, PARA** ($C_{10}H_{14}O$; a flammable hydrocarbon solvent). Used in citrus and spice flavorings for beverages, ice cream, ices, candy, baked goods, chewing gum, and condiments. Contact with the liquid may cause blisters of the skin and inflammation of mucous membranes. Ingestion of excessive amounts may be followed by a burning sensation in the mouth and stomach, nausea, vomiting, headache, confusion, and coma. Also called benzyl alcohol.

# D

**2,4-D.** See **2,4-DICHLOROPHENOXYACETIC ACID.**

**DAMINOZIDE** $(C_6H_{12}N_2O_3)$. Used on apples, peanuts, and other crops to delay ripening. For some time it has been known that daminozide causes several types of cancer in rats and mice. Data collected in August 1985 indicate that daminozide remains on the produce and may be carcinogenic in humans. The EPA is considering a ban on its manufacture and use.

**DBCP.** See **DIBROMO-3-CHLOROPROPANE.**

**DBDO.** See **DECABROMODIPHENYL OXIDE.**

**DDT** $(C_{14}H_9Cl_5$; a white crystalline solid; standard 1 mg/m$^3$). DDT is an acronym for *d*ichloro*d*iphenyl*t*richloroethane. Used chiefly as a "miracle" insecticide of World War II to control typhus- and malaria-carrying insects in tropical areas, DDT reached its peak agricultural use in 1959.

DDT can cause serious damage to the nervous system and is considered poisonous to warm-blooded animals. The substance persists in the environment, accumulates in the food chain, causes reproductive failure in birds and fish, and collects in the fat cells of humans and animals. Tests conducted from 1947 to 1969 showed DDT to be carcinogenic in animals.

DDT was banned for use in the United States in 1972, but traces of it still remain in the environment, a situation that puts the entire population at risk. Estimates set an estimated

DDT level in the general population of the United States at 16.7 ppb. In 1981 the EPA found concentrations of DDT 80 times above federal standards in the drinking water of the Texas Rio Grande Valley. In 1977 a fish caught in a creek in Triana, Alabama, near the site of a plant that manufactured DDT until 1970 had 500 ppm in its flesh. One 85-year-old man living nearby had 3,000 ppb in his blood—the highest recorded concentration in a human. (8, 11)

**DECABORANE** ($B_{10}H_{14}$; a flammable solid; standard 0.3 mg/m$^3$). Used as a gasoline additive and in the manufacture of rocket propellants. It affects the central nervous system, causing neurological and behavioral disturbances.

**DECABROMODIPHENYL OXIDE (DBDO)** ($C_{12}Br_{10}O$). A toxic substance that is related to PCBs and PBBs. It is used as a flame retardant in plastics. DBDO is highly toxic and persistent in the environment.

**DIAMINE.** See **HYDRAZINE.**

**DIBROMOCHLOROPROPANE (DBCP)** ($C_3H_5Br_2Cl$; a dense yellow liquid with a pungent odor; standard 1 ppb). Used chiefly as a pesticide between 1957 and 1977. In the summer of 1977 several workers at an Occidental Petroleum Company plant in Lathrop, California, found in casual conversation that none of their wives were able to become pregnant. Tests showed that 35 of the 114 workers were sterile. A Dow Chemical Plant in Magnolia, Arkansas, found that 62 of 86 workers were either sterile or had a very low sperm count. As a result of other investigations, it was found that about one-third of all workers exposed to the substance were sterile. In August 1977 production was stopped, and the standard of 1 ppb was set. By 1979, high levels of DBCP were still found in about 2,000 wells in California. In addition to infertility, workers were found to suffer kidney and liver damage as well. There is also some suspicion that DBCP might be carcinogenic. (11)

**DICHLORODIPHENYLTRICHLOROETHANE.** See **DDT.**

**2,4-DICHLOROPHENOXYACETIC ACID (2,4-D)** $(C_8 H_6 Cl_2 O_3$ ; a colorless nonflammable powder; standard 10 mg/m$^3$). Among the most widely used weed killers or herbicides. The dust of 2,4-D is irritating to the respiratory passages. Tests show that it causes paralysis, neuritis, reproduction damage, and cancer of the lymph glands and mammaries in animals. Users of this substance suffer from weakness, muscle twitching, convulsions, and dermatitis. (11)

**DIELDRIN** $(C_{12} H_8 Cl_6 O$; a light-tan nonflammable crystalline solid; standard 0.25 mg/m$^3$). Introduced in 1948, this acutely toxic insecticide was restricted in 1974. Studies found the substance present in 96 percent of all meat, fish, poultry, 90 percent of all air samples, and in the flesh of 99.5 percent of all Americans. Dieldrin remains in the soil and persists in the food chain. In humans, it affects the central nervous system, liver, kidneys, and skin, and is believed to be carcinogenic. The substance is toxic to organisms that live in water and also accumulates in their bodies. Evidence shows that it is linked to reproductive failure in birds and fish. (11)

**DIOXIN.** A group of about 75 compounds that are considered by a number of scientists as highly poisonous chemicals. The most toxic of the dioxins is believed to be tetrachlorodioxin (TCDD). (It is believed that less than three ounces of TCDD could kill the entire population of New York City.) Dioxin was first produced and used as a pesticide and weed killer in the United States in 1948. It is also created as an unwanted by-product in the manufacture of several other pesticides and herbicides as well as in the burning of paper, wood, and plastic. (A $135 million incinerator on Long Island was closed in 1980 after just one year of use when it was found to be emitting dioxin in its smoke.) People are exposed to dioxin in the manufacture and use of the various herbicides in which it is a contaminant, by living near such plants or fields, by eating foods that have been sprayed with these products, or by breathing the air after spraying or the improper burning of waste products.

Many experimental and epidemiological studies have been done on dioxin. In the laboratory, it was found that dioxin at a level of just a few parts per trillion killed guinea pigs, caused cancer in mice, and led to reproductive damage in rodents, cattle, and monkeys. In 1978 Swedish researchers reported that lumberjacks exposed to dioxin had up to six times as many soft-tissue cancers as would be expected. And in America in 1983 NIOSH released figures showing seven workers with soft-tissue cancers in a group of 4,000 heavily exposed to dioxin. The average rate is 1 in 7,000. The most common result of exposure to dioxin is a skin condition known as chloracne. Other complaints are cirrhosis of the liver, nervous disorders, depression, and the inability to bear heat.

It is estimated that about 15 million pounds of herbicides containing dioxin have been sprayed on approximately 2 million acres in the United States. Further, thousands of American servicemen were exposed to dioxin when they participated in the spraying of the defoliant Agent Orange in Vietnam from 1965 to 1970.

In 1963 in Amsterdam a plant making an herbicide in which dioxin appeared as a contaminant exploded. Six months later, 18 workers entered the ruins of the plant to start the clean-up process. They wore deep-sea diving suits, face masks, and eye goggles. Nine of the men developed chloracne, three died within two years, and the one man who did not wear a face mask and goggles was paralyzed in the legs.

In 1976 a chemical plant in Seveso, Italy, exploded, sending a great cloud of dioxin gas into the air. Many of the people near the accident suffered burns and sores on their skin; there was also an increase in physical and personality changes: large numbers of people became more nervous, excessively tired, moody, irritable, and lost their appetite. Of the women in the area who were pregnant at the time, 90 had medical abortions and 51 attempting to go to term had spontaneous abortions. Uncounted numbers of farm, wild, and pet animals were killed, many with severe liver damage. Over 80,000 domestic animals were slaughtered as a protective measure.

The EPA has not set a standard for dioxin, claiming that the only adverse human effect is chloracne. (In Canada, the Ministry of the Environment in Ontario set a standard of 30 trillionths of a gram/m$^3$.) Scientists are not in agreement on dioxin. Dr. Bertram Carnow, of the University of Illinois College of Medicine, says it is wrong to assume that there is any safe level of dioxin, while Dr. Lewis Thomas, president of Memorial Sloan-Kettering Cancer Center, says there is no proof that dioxin causes cancer in humans. Nevertheless, in 1970 the Agriculture Department banned most uses of dioxin, and in 1979 the EPA suspended the use of 2,4,5-T, the herbicide that contains dioxin, except on rangelands and rice fields. Studies are continuing to determine the true toxicity of dioxin. See also **AGENT ORANGE** and **TIMES BEACH.** (11)

**DUST.** Fine particles of cotton, coal, or other material light enough to be suspended in air.

# E

**EBDC.** See **ETHYLENE BIS(DITHIOCARBAMATE).**

**EDB.** See **ETHYLENE DIBROMIDE.**

**EDTA.** See **ETHYLENE DIAMINE TETRAACETATE.**

**ENDRIN** ($C_2H_2Cl_6O$; a white crystalline solid; standard 0.1 mg/m$^3$). Used as a pesticide, it is related to DDT, but is much more toxic. The substance is known to attack the central nervous system and liver, causing nausea, mental disorientation, and convulsions. It is also a carcinogen, can lead to birth defects, and has been known to cause death by respiratory failure. One-quarter of an ounce can kill a human. In the sheikdom of Qatar, during June and July 1967, 700 victims were hospitalized and 24 died after eating bread made with flour that arrived by ship from Houston, Texas, where endrin had accidentally been mixed in with the flour. In 1976, endrin was sprayed over Kansas; 2 million fish and 20 cattle were killed, and 8,000 pounds of milk had to be discarded. Currently, there are some restrictions on its use in agriculture, but there is no EPA ban.(11)

**EPICHLOROHYDRIN** ($C_3H_5ClO$; a colorless flammable liquid with a chloroformlike irritating odor; standard 5 ppm). Used to condition starches in food processing. The vapors of this toxic material are irritating to the eyes, nose, and throat. Chronic poisoning symptoms include great weariness, disturbances of the gastrointestinal tract, severe eye irritation, and kidney damage.

**EPOXY.** A class of substances used chiefly in adhesives, coatings, electrical insulation, solder mix, and as protection for computer circuit boards. The materials are suspected of causing cancer.

**ETHYL ACRYLATE** ($C_5 H_8 O_2$ ; a colorless liquid; standard 25 ppm). Used in the manufacture of water-resistant paint, paper coating, and leather finishes. Also used in fruit, liquor, and rum flavorings for beverages, ice cream, candy, baked goods, and chewing gum. The substance can be very irritating to the eyes, skin, and mucous membranes. Inhalation of the vapors can cause lethargy or convulsions. Chronic intake may damage the heart, kidney, or spleen. Also called ethyl propionate.

**ETHYLENE BIS(DITHIOCARBAMATE) (EBDC)** ($C_4 H_6 N_2 S_4$). Used as a pesticide on potatoes, tomatoes, mushrooms, cucumbers, bananas, and many other fruits and vegetables. It leaves a residue that causes cancer and other diseases in animals.

**ETHYLENE CHLORIDE.** See **ETHYLENE DICHLORIDE.**

**ETHYLENE DIAMINE TETRAACETATE (EDTA)** ($C_{10} H_{16} N_2 O_8$ ; a flammable liquid with an ammonia odor). Food manufacturers use EDTA to trap and remove tiny particles of metal that enter the food from the rollers, scrapers, and blenders, with which food is processed. Other uses for the substance include the processing of salad dressings, mayonnaise, fruits and vegetables, fruit juices, shellfish, beer, and soda. Doctors inject patients suffering from metal poisoning with the substance. The liquid and vapor are dangerous to the eyes, and it has a caustic effect on body tissues and mucous membranes. EDTA is on the FDA list of substances to be studied for possible harmful effects.

**ETHYLENE DIBROMIDE (EDB)** ($C_2H_4Br_2$; a colorless highly toxic flammable liquid; standard 20 ppm). Used to protect citrus fruits from fruit flies. Most EDB, though, is added to leaded gasoline to prevent engine knocking. Chemical manufacturers use it as a solvent for resins, gums, and waxes. The liquid and vapor are very dangerous to the eyes and can cause fatal liver damage. In 1975 and 1977, National Cancer Institute studies showed that high doses induced cancer in laboratory animals; it is believed to be a carcinogen in humans as well. A 1980 EPA study disclosed the possible contamination of fruit and grain fumigated with EDB while in storage. In 1983 it was found to be responsible for serious groundwater contamination in Georgia, California, Hawaii, and Florida. At greatest risk are an estimated 108,000 workers who produce EDB and 875,000 who are exposed to leaded gasoline. In 1983 the EPA banned EDB for soil fumigation and set limits on EDB residues in baking mixes, cereals, and snack foods. In 1984 the substance was banned for most food use. Its only present applications are in fumigating fresh fruit to kill fruit flies and as a gasoline additive.

**ETHYLENE DICHLORIDE** ($C_2H_4Cl_2$; a colorless flammable liquid having a chloroform odor; standard 50 ppm). Used as a pesticide and in the manufacture of synthetics and plastics. It is toxic if inhaled, ingested, or brought into long or repeated contact with the skin. Animal studies show that prolonged exposure may cause liver, kidney, and digestive disorders. Exposed workers suffer nausea, confusion, dizziness, liver and kidney damage. Acute effects include neurological damage, and death from respiratory or circulatory failure. The EPA banned the use of ethylene dichloride as a pesticide in December 1985. Also called ethylene chloride or glycol dichloride.

**ETHYLENE OXIDE (ETO)** ($C_2H_4O$; a colorless flammable liquid with an etherlike smell; standard 50 ppm). Among the

25 most widely used chemicals, with over 2 million tons produced annually in the United States. Its vapors form explosive mixtures with air at all temperatures down to 20°F, making it a dangerous fire hazard. Most of the ETO that is produced is used in the production of ethylene glycol, a major part of antifreeze, and for polyester fibers, films, and bottles. Its other uses include the manufacture of laundry and dishwashing detergents and substances for sterilizing and fumigating. Both liquid and vapors can seriously irritate the eyes and damage the kidneys. The substance has also been linked to leukemia and other cancers and to reproductive damage. An estimated 140,000 workers are exposed through manufacture; many others also have contact with this material when it is used as a sterilant in hospitals. EPA studies show that nearly 2 out of every 1,000 people continuously exposed to ETO will fall ill with cancer, and that about 58 cases of cancer annually are directly caused by ETO. The EPA, therefore, listed ethylene oxide as a hazardous substance in September 1985. Also called oxirane. (25)

**ETHYL FORMATE** ($C_3H_6O_2$ ; a colorless flammable liquid with a distinct odor; standard 100 ppm). Used as a yeast and mold inhibitor. It is also a fumigant for raisins and currants and a fungicide for cashew nuts, cereals, tobacco, and dried fruits. In many foods it gives an artificial blueberry, raspberry, strawberry, apple, banana, cherry, or other flavoring. Its vapors cause irritation and narcosis, even after short periods of exposure. In heavy concentrations it paralyzes the central nervous system, resulting in death. Also called formic ether.

**ETHYL NITRITE** ($C_2H_5NO_2$ ; colorless to yellow flammable liquid with an etherlike smell). Used as a synthetic flavoring agent in beverages, ice cream, ices, candy, baked goods, and chewing gum. Its vapors form explosive mixtures with air at temperatures down to $-31°F$. Excessive exposure may cause methemoglobinemia, a disease in which oxygen is diminished in red blood cells, and low blood pressure.

**ETHYL PROPIONATE.** See **ETHYL ACRYLATE.**

**ETO.** See **ETHYLENE OXIDE.**

**EUCALYPTUS OIL.** Used as an expectorant, as an intestinal dewormer, and as a local antiseptic. It is also found as flavoring in beverages, ice cream, ices, candy, baked goods, and liquors. The sensitivity to eucalyptus varies, but ingestion of as little as 3 milliliters can produce a burning sensation, with nausea, weakness, and delirium following. Coma and fatalities have sometimes occurred after comparatively small amounts were taken.

# f

**FLUE GAS.** The pollutants emitted to the atmosphere after combustion or some production process takes place. Also called stack gas.

**FLUE GAS DESULFURIZATION.** Any pollution control process that removes sulfur oxides from flue gas.

**FLUE GAS SCRUBBER.** Equipment used to remove fly ash or other objectionable materials from flue gas through the use of sprays, wet baffles, or other means. Also called flue gas washer, gas scrubber, or gas washer.

**FLUOROCARBONS.** See **CHLOROFLUOROCARBONS.**

**FOOD COLORS.** Additives used to color many different food products. There are seven food colors or food dyes now in use. They are all made from coal tar and are identified by the color name and a number. Americans consumed over 6 million pounds of these dyes in 1984. In order of use they are

Red 40 (2,630,000 pounds). Used in candy, desserts, and baked goods. It can cause lymph tumors. The substance is banned in several European countries.

Yellow 5 (1,620,000 pounds). Used in bottled drinks, baked goods, and pet foods. It can cause allergies, thyroid and lymph tumors, and chromosomal damage. Currently, it is illegal to use the material in Norway.

Yellow 6 (1,530,000 pounds). Used in bottled drinks, candy, desserts, and sausage. It can cause allergies, kidney tumors, and chromosomal damage. In Norway and Sweden it is against the law for Yellow 6 to be used in food manufacture.

Blue 1 (260,400 pounds). Used in bottled drinks, candy, and baked goods. It can cause chromosomal damage and is not allowed in French and Finnish food products.

Red 3 (241,300 pounds). Used in candy, desserts, and baked goods. It can cause thyroid tumors and chromosomal damage.

Blue 2 (101,000 pounds). Used in candy, bottled drinks, and pet foods. It can cause brain tumors. Norway forbids its use.

Green 3 (3,600 pounds). Used in bottled drinks and candy. It can cause bladder tumors and has been outlawed in several European countries.

**FORMALDEHYDE** ($CH_2O$; a colorless flammable pungent gas; standard 3 ppm). Mostly used in the manufacture of textiles, plastics, building materials, insulation products, auto parts, and fungicides, and as a disinfectant and preservative. It does damage by tying together strands of DNA. Workers who inhale the fumes or have skin contact with formalin (formaldehyde in a water solution) suffer irritation of the lungs or skin. Formaldehyde is known to cause cancer in laboratory rats, and 1975 studies also show an increase in cancer among exposed workers. More than one million workers are exposed through the manufacture and use of formaldehyde; millions are exposed to low levels because they live near the manufacturing plants. In 1970 OSHA set limits on acceptable amounts of exposure. Early in 1986 OSHA held hearings in response to lowering the standard to either 1 or 1.5 ppm. The CSPC requires a label warning of "strong sensitizer" on some household products, and in 1982 banned the use of urea-formaldehyde home insulation. The next year the ban was overturned, but little of the product is now marketed. Also called methanal, formol, or formalin.

**FORMALIN.** See **FORMALDEHYDE.**

**FORMIC ACID** ($CH_2O_2$; a colorless flammable liquid with a pungent odor; standard 5 ppm). Originally prepared from red ants. Synthetic formic acid now is used to dissolve the bones and remove the hair from animal bodies. It is also found in fruit flavoring for beverages, ice cream, ices, candy, and baked goods. A corrosive liquid, it produces violent burns and blisters on contact. When ingested in large quantities, it induces nephritis. Also called methanoic acid.

**FORMIC ETHER.** See **ETHYL FORMATE.**

**FORMOL.** See **FORMALDEHYDE.**

**FREON.** See **CHLOROFLUOROCARBONS.**

**FUMING TIN CHLORIDE.** See **STANNOUS CHLORIDE.**

# G

**GARLIC OIL.** See **ALLYL SULFIDE.**

**GASOLINE.** Used mainly as a fuel for internal combustion engines and as a solvent. A toxic substance, it is a volatile, flammable liquid mixture of hydrocarbons obtained from petroleum. Gasoline may be swallowed accidentally (when siphoning), absorbed through the skin (when used to wash motor parts), or inhaled. The substance acts as a depressant on the central nervous system. The first symptoms are flushing, staggering, slurred speech, and confusion. Unconsciousness, coma, and death may result from overexposure. Gasoline is called petrol in England.

**GLYCOL DICHLORIDE.** See **ETHYLENE DICHLORIDE.**

**GLYCOL ETHERS.** A group of four chemicals—ethoxyethanol, methoxyethanol, and their acetates. They are used in tens of thousands of products, including paints, stains, varnishes, and solvents. Electronic companies use glycol ethers as solvents in the manufacture of computer chips. About 220 million pounds were manufactured in 1983. In 1929 the glycol ethers were found to retard growth and induce birth defects in animal fetuses. In 1938 they were linked to blood and nervous disorders. In 1982 it was found that inhaling glycol ethers or skin contact with these substances could be poisonous to human fetuses.

**GRAIN ELEVATOR DUST.** Dust that is created as grain is stored, handled, or moved. A flame or hot ash (cigarettes, matches, lighters), spark (parts of machinery, electrical switches), or heated surface (light bulb, radiators, electrical appliances) can ignite the dust and cause an explosion. Welding to repair the metal of the grain elevator is the major single cause (about 10 percent) of explosions of grain elevator dust. If grain is moist (about 20 percent by weight), decomposition occurs, producing methanol, propanol, and butanol, which are flammable. Fumigants, too, contain flammable ingredients that add to the hazard.

**GREEN 3.** See **FOOD COLORS.**

**HAIR DYES.** Hair coloring preparations used by 33 million men and women, mostly at home. These substances usually contain 4-methoxy-m-phenylenediamine (4-MMPD). In 1977 the National Cancer Institute reported a link between 4-MMPD and cancer of the breast and bladder. In 1979 the FDA proposed a regulation requiring a warning label on preparations containing the suspected carcinogen. The regulation was challenged and a stay was issued. The regulation is not yet in effect. Currently, some manufacturers have voluntarily withheld 4-MMPD from their products.

**HCB.** See **HEXACHLOROBENZENE.**

**HEAT.** Found in bakeries, steel mills, laundries, food canneries, and brick and ceramics factories. It causes not only discomfort but also health risks. In extreme heat, more blood goes to the body surface and less to the active muscles, resulting in a decline in strength and an increase in fatigue. In addition, there are psychological effects; accuracy, comprehension, and memory suffer. More accidents are reported because of loss of mental ability, as well as from slippery palms, dizziness, and fogged glasses. Heat stroke, caused by loss of fluid and salt in sweating, is perhaps the most serious health problem. In heat stroke the body system for dealing with heat breaks down; the skin is hot, dry, and red; the person is confused and irritable. If not removed from heat, unconsciousness, delirium, and convulsions may occur and may lead to death. Heat cramps, which are painful spasms in the muscles of the arms, legs, and abdomen, may also occur in exposed workers. (45)

**HEAVY METALS.** Metallic elements with high molecular weights such as mercury, chromium, cadmium, arsenic, and lead. They can damage living things at even low concentrations and tend to accumulate in the food chain.

**HEMATITE** ($Fe_2O_3$; the principal ore of iron). It occurs in steel-gray to black crystals and in red earthy masses. Hematite may be linked to lung cancer in miners.

**HEXACHLOROBENZENE (HCB)** ($C_6Cl_6$; a crystalline powder; standard 50 ppm). Used as a fungicide. This material is harmful to the respiratory system, the eyes, and the liver. In the late 1950s, some 3,000 Turkish children ate bread contaminated with hexachlorobenzene. Reports indicated that their growth was stunted, their skin was darkened, they had a sensitivity to light, and they showed unusual hair growth on their faces. Also called perchlorobenzene.

**HEXANONE-2.** See **METHYL BUTYL KETONE.**

**HEXONE.** See **METHYL ISOBUTYL KETONE.**

**HIGH DENSITY POLYETHYLENE.** A material used to make plastic bottles. The substance produces toxic fumes when it is burned.

**HYDRAZINE** ($N_2H_4$; a colorless oily flammable liquid; standard 1 ppm). Used chiefly as a reducing agent and jet fuel. About 100,000 workers are exposed to this substance. Its highly irritating fumes attack the eyes and skin, causing temporary blindness and skin burns. Chronic exposure may result in liver and kidney damage. In animals, hydrazine has been linked to liver and lung cancer. Also called diamine.

**HYDROCARBON.** Any one of a family of compounds containing carbon and hydrogen in various combinations. This includes four major classes of compounds: alkanes, alkenes, naphthenes, and aromatics. Each has its own characteristic structural arrangement of hydrogen and carbon atoms, as well as different physical and chemical properties. Hydrocarbons are the principal constituents of crude oil, natural gas, and refined petroleum products. Some of the hydrocarbon compounds are major air pollutants; they may be carcinogenic or play an active role in changing substances in the presence of sunlight. See also **ALKANES, ALKENES, AROMATICS,** and **NAPHTHENES.**

**HYDROFLUORIC ACID.** See **HYDROGEN FLUORIDE.**

**HYDROGEN CYANIDE** (HCN: a liquid or flammable gas with a faint odor; standard 10 ppm). Used chiefly as a fumigant. It is generated in blast furnaces, gas works, and coke ovens. It also may be produced in chemical laboratories if a cyanide salt is contacted by an acid solution. The vapors are intensely poisonous and highly flammable. High concentrations cause giddiness, headache, unconsciousness, and convulsions, with cessation of respiration very likely. Lower concentrations cause irritation of the throat, difficulty in breathing, and watering of the eyes. Also called prussic acid.

**HYDROGEN FLUORIDE** (HF; a colorless liquid or gas; standard 3 ppm). Used in the manufacture of several chemical products and in the etching of glass. It is a corrosive liquid that is highly toxic. Small amounts in the eyes can cause intense irritation; large amounts, immediate blindness. The vapor or liquid is very dangerous when in contact with the skin or if ingested. On the skin it can cause painful burns. If swallowed, it causes severe irritation to the esophagus and stomach. In contact with metals, this substance is corrosive and produces hydrogen gas, which is an explosive hazard. Also called hydrofluoric acid.

**HYDROGEN PHOSPHIDE.** See **PHOSPHINE.**

**HYDROGEN SULFIDE** ($H_2S$; a colorless flammable gas having the odor of rotten eggs; standard 20 ppm). Used chiefly in the manufacture of chemicals, in metallurgy, and as a reagent in laboratory analysis. This substance is irritating to the eyes and respiratory tissues. Increasing concentrations become more and more harmful; acute exposure results in coma and death from respiratory failure. Its very characteristic smell is not reliable as a warning signal because high concentrations destroy the sense of smell.

**HYDROXYTOLUENE.** See **BENZYL ALCOHOL.**

**I**

**INDOOR POLLUTION.** The contamination of indoor air, particularly in houses and apartments, by a number of hazardous pollutants. The principal ones are radon (from the soil and building materials), asbestos (from building materials and certain appliances), particles (from tobacco smoke, oil burners, and fireplaces), carbon monoxide and nitrogen dioxide (from gas stoves), formaldehyde (from insulation, plywood, particle board, foam, and home furnishings), hydrocarbons (from paint, varnish, and cleaning sprays), and benzene, styrene, carbon tetrachloride, and chloroform found in several household products.

Over the last decade the problem of indoor pollution has grown much worse. Many homeowners have sealed, caulked, and insulated their houses in order to cut down air leaks and save energy. In some cases, the insulation itself is a source of pollution. Further, a number of newer buildings were constructed with windows that do not open and the old air is recirculated to keep down heating and air conditioning expenses. As a result, the pollutants are trapped in the living areas where people spend up to 90 percent of their time.

In a 1985 study the EPA reported that the level of hazardous pollutants in indoor air can be as much as 70 times higher than in outdoor air. Indoor concentrations of radon, for example, are frequently ten times greater; nitrogen dioxide from gas stoves sometimes exceeds outdoor air quality standards. Some of the symptoms of indoor air pollution are headache, nausea, dizziness, drowsiness, breathing difficulty, coughing, rashes, insomnia, lethargy, loss of memory, and irritations to the eyes, nose, and throat. According to the Consumer Federation of America, indoor pollution causes $100 billion in medical expenses and lost productivity.

A National Academy of Sciences panel advised reducing indoor pollution by using different building and furnishing materials and by increasing the amount of ventilation. It also suggested that it was the responsibility of individuals, manufacturers, building designers, and contractors, as well as government, to take action on this issue. See also **ASBESTOS, RADIO-ACTIVE SUBSTANCES,** and **FORMALDEHYDE.**

**IODOMETHANE.** See **METHYL IODIDE.**

# K

**KEPONE** ($C_{10}Cl_{10}O$; a crystalline solid; no federal standard). Used chiefly as a pesticide against fire ants and in cockroach traps; also found in agriculture. In 1975 a Virginia doctor noticed several symptoms of neurological disease among kepone production workers, which led to a program of animal testing. In 1976, NIOSH reported that kepone causes cancer in rats. By then, production of the chemical had been halted, and fishing was banned in Virginia's James River and the lower Chesapeake Bay. But already about 75 workers, 10 of their spouses, and many of their children were suffering from kepone poisoning. Twenty-nine were hospitalized with brain and liver damage, tremors, blurred vision, skin discoloration, joint and chest pains, anxiety, memory loss, twitching eyes, and slurred speech. Fourteen workers became sterile.

For five years no fishing was allowed in the area. But then, in response to pressure from the fishing industry, the government allowed fishing again, even though the kepone level was still high.

**KETONE PROPANE. See ACETONE.**

# L

**LEAD** (Pb; a soft, bluish-gray metallic element; standard 0.05 mg/m$^3$). Used as a gasoline additive, as a base for paints, in storage batteries, as the solder to seal tin cans, as a shield and absorber of neutrons in nuclear reactors, and in many other applications. The lead in gasoline is a threat to the general population. People living in areas subject to acid rain have found lead from their water pipes leaching into their drinking water. Many children have been poisoned by eating or licking chips of lead-based paints. And, of course, all those involved in the mining, smelting, processing, and manufacturing of lead products are at risk as well.

Lead attacks the kidneys, the blood, and the nervous system. The range of symptoms includes convulsions, anemia, miscarriages, birth defects, hearing loss, disorders in eye-hand coordination, depression, and anxiety. Exposure to high levels of lead can cause severe learning disabilities in young children. The substance is toxic to domestic plants and animals; it becomes more concentrated the higher up it is found in the food chain.

The present law forbids the use of lead as a gasoline additive after 1992, but the EPA seems to be inclining toward an earlier ban. The present limit is 1.1 grams per gallon. Leaded gasoline is already banned in Germany, and England is moving in that direction as well.

**LEAD ARSENATE** (PbHAsO$_4$; white powder; standard 0.05 mg/m$^3$). Used as an insecticide and to treat tapeworms in animals. Lead arsenate can enter the body through inhalation, ingestion, or skin contact. Among the symptoms of exposure are nausea, diarrhea, skin inflammation, abdominal pain, loss of appetite, tiredness, and weakness.

**LEPTOPHOS** ($C_{13}H_{10}BrCl_2O_2PS$). Used as an insecticide and pesticide from around 1970 to 1976, when production was stopped. It affected both the workers in the plants manufacturing the chemical and the agricultural workers who applied it to the crops. Leptophos causes severe neurological damage, with symptoms similar to that of multiple sclerosis. Workers who were exposed to the substance showed signs of weakness, tremors, numbness, tingling, blurred vision, temporary memory loss, and paralysis of the legs.

In a plant producing leptophos in Bayport, Texas, one 33-year-old worker, a former paratrooper, developed difficulty in walking and talking; his weight dropped from 140 to 110 pounds. Another worker in the same plant was admitted to a mental hospital where he was described as "disoriented, unable to walk without staggering, having auditory hallucinations, and wandering around aimlessly."

**LINDANE** ($C_6H_6Cl_6$; a white crystalline powder; standard 0.5 mg/m$^3$). Named after the Dutch chemist T. van der Linden, lindane is an insecticide and weed killer. It is the most widely used of indoor insecticides, with production running at about 900,000 pounds per year and some 126 million Americans exposed. The results of exposure to lindane range from headaches, nausea, depression, and respiratory difficulties from low-level exposure, to convulsions, raised white blood cell count, and heart failure in severe cases. It is also linked to cancer and birth defects. Children seem particularly vulnerable to the toxic effects of lindane.

The government has now banned the use of lindane on stored foodstuffs because it leaves a poisonous residue; its use is restricted to pretreating seeds for planting. In September 1984 the EPA agreed to do a more complete study on the effects of lindane. (11)

**LOVE CANAL CHEMICALS.** Described as the largest man-made environmental disaster, Love Canal is a 16-acre landfill site near the city of Niagara Falls, New York. From the 1920s until the 1950s, Love Canal was used as a chemical waste dump by the Hooker Chemical and Plastics Corporation. It is estimated that nearly 22,000 tons of waste chemicals were deposited on this site. In 1953, Hooker sold the land to the Niagara Falls Board of Education, which covered over the land and built an elementary school there. Private developers also moved in and built 1,000 small single-family homes.

By the 1970s it was obvious that something was seriously wrong at Love Canal. Children playing in their backyards developed skin rashes and saw the dark, oozy soil burn holes in their sneakers. The few trees that were growing in the neighborhood turned black, and there was a pervasive stench in the air.

But perhaps most frightening of all was the deteriorating health of the residents. Of 17 pregnant women living in Love Canal, only 2 had normal births; there were 4 miscarriages, 2 stillbirths, and 9 children born with birth defects. In the 15 homes on 96th Street alone there were 6 cases of breast cancer, 1 throat cancer, and 1 bladder cancer.

In 1978 President Carter declared Love Canal a disaster area, and New York State closed the school and evacuated the 239 families living there. (1, 3, 11)

**MALATHION**  $(C_{10}H_{19}O_6PS_2$ ; a yellow liquid; standard 15 mg/m$^3$). A chemical trademark for an organic phosphorus compound that is used as an insecticide. Malathion is used to control insects on fruits and vegetables, and flies, lice, and mosquitoes on farm and livestock animals. About 75,000 workers are exposed, either through manufacture or application. In 1982 and again in 1984 Malathion was sprayed by helicopters in California in an attempt to rid the crops of the Mexican fruit fly. According to the National Cancer Institute and the Centers for Disease Control, there is no danger from Malathion. Yet the John Muir Institute for Environmental Studies, two doctors at Harvard Medical School, and several others suggest that Malathion does attack the liver, blood, central nervous system, and gastrointestinal tract. The symptoms they cite are nausea, vomiting, sweating, and weakness. Some studies also find that it alters brain waves, leading to insomnia and irritability.

**MANGANESE** (Mn; a metallic element; standard 5 mg/m$^3$). Miners and smelters are exposed as well as workers in the steel, ceramics, and welding industries and those involved in the manufacture of drugs, glass, paint, varnish, and ink. Manganese dust and fumes are minor irritants to the eyes and respiratory tract. Chronic exposure, however, affects the blood and body organs, especially the liver and spleen, and certain nerve cells. The first symptoms are apathy, anorexia, headache, weak legs, and irritability. Manganese psychosis follows: unaccountable laughter, euphoria, impulsive acts, confusion, aggressiveness, and hallucinations. Other symptoms include speech disturbances, masklike face, difficulties in gait and balance, and tremors. Although death from manganese poisoning is unusual, the effects can be very disabling. Unless this condition is caught early and treated, it may become permanent.

**MENTHOL** ($C_{10}H_{20}O$; a colorless crystalline solid). Obtained from peppermint oil or synthesized, it is used chiefly in perfumes, confections, liqueurs, and in medicine for colds and nasal disorders because of its cooling effect on mucous membranes. If ingested in its concentrated form, it can cause severe abdominal pain, nausea, vomiting, and coma. It has also been known to cause severe eye injuries. Also called peppermint camphor.

**MERCURY** (Hg; a liquid metallic element; standard 1 mg/m$^3$). Used in thermometers and barometers, pesticides, drugs, dental fillings, mirror backings, electrical switches, dry cell batteries, fluorescent lights, and in the production of chlorine and other chemical products. It is placed in dry cell batteries to prevent corrosion, added to paints to resist mildew, and mixed in with seeds as a fungicide. Worldwide production of mercury has doubled since World War II. The vapor is dangerous, and although the mercury can enter the body through the skin or mouth, inhalation is most frequent. Even a short exposure to a high level of colorless, odorless mercury vapor can result in acute poisoning with chest pain, difficulty in breathing, inflammation of mouth and gums, fever, and headache. But long exposure to low levels of mercury is much more common. The effects on the central nervous system produce tremors or shaking, particularly of the hands. Also, personality changes occur, including irritability, temper outbursts, excitability, shyness, and indecision. Some people show slowed reaction time and an inability to perform delicate tasks.

During the 1950s and 1960s thousands of people who lived around Minamata Bay in Japan were paralyzed, crippled, or killed from eating fish contaminated by mercury wastes that several chemical plants had dumped into the water. A new problem with mercury in Japan in the 1980s is the disposal of used batteries. In 1983, for example, 2.85 billion batteries were produced and thrown away when dead. The mercury from all these batteries seeps into the soil around garbage dumps, poisoning the underground water and the nearby soil. There is now a move on in Japan to collect old batteries separate from all other garbage. (48)

**METHANAL.** See **FORMALDEHYDE.**

**METHANOIC ACID.** See **FORMIC ACID.**

**METHANOL** ($CH_4O$; a colorless flammable liquid; standard 200 ppm). Used for chemical manufacture and as a solvent. A toxic material, it is found in paint, varnish removers, and cleaning fluids. Contact with the skin can cause a mild dermatitis. But swallowing or long-term, high-concentration contact may lead to central nervous system damage. The kidneys, liver, heart, and other organs may also be affected. The symptoms of headache, nausea, giddiness, and loss of consciousness may appear 9 to 36 hours after exposure. Optic nerve damage and blindness are the result of severe poisoning from this material. About 175,000 workers use this substance. Also called methyl alcohol or wood alcohol.

**METHYL ACRYLATE** ($C_4H_6O_2$; a waterlike flammable liquid; standard 10 ppm). Used in packaging and to coat paper and plastic film. It can be highly irritating to the eyes, skin, and mucous membranes. If vapors are inhaled in high concentration, convulsions will occur.

**METHYL ALCOHOL.** See **METHANOL.**

**METHYL BROMIDE** ($CH_3 Br$; a colorless poisonous gas; standard 20 ppm). Used chiefly in drug manufacture and as a fumigant in soil and in grain storage warehouses. It is also used as a pesticide against fruit flies in shipments of citrus. Methyl bromide is applied after the fruit is boxed and loaded, making the skin of the fruit look pitted and waxy. Scientists have found that the substance produces cancer in animals. Workers who use this material may suffer irritations of the eyes, skin, mucous membranes, and upper respiratory system. The first symptoms, which occur one-half to six hours after exposure, include visual problems, headache, nausea, vomiting, and tremors, followed by coma and death due to respiratory or circulatory failure. If the victim survives, permanent kidney or brain damage may result. Low-level chronic poisoning affects the central nervous system and causes lethargy, muscle pains, visual and speech disturbances as well as confusion. Also called bromomethane.

**METHYL BUTYL KETONE** ($C_6 H_{12} O$; a colorless flammable liquid; standard 100 ppm). Used to make solvents, varnish and stain products, waxes, adhesives, explosives, celluloid, dyes, oils, and lacquers. Nearly 300,000 workers are exposed in the various industries manufacturing these products. The material attacks the central nervous system, the skin, and the respiratory system. In addition to irritation of the eyes and nose, workers may develop weakness, dermatitis, headaches, and drowsiness. Also called hexanone-2.

**METHYL CHLORIDE** ($CH_3 Cl$; a colorless flammable gas; standard 100 ppm). Used in petroleum refineries, synthetic rubber plants, and in drug manufacture. Also used as a refrigerant and as a local anesthetic (it freezes tissue). Because of its use as refrigerant, methyl chloride is a danger to repairmen and other maintenance workers who handle leaky refrigerators, for example. The substance is a known carcinogen in animals. It attacks the liver, kidney, skin, and central nervous system in humans and can actually cause frostbite to the eyes. Overexposure results in a staggering gait, speech difficulties, nausea, headache, dizziness, and blurred vision. High doses can cause convulsions and coma. Also called chloromethane.

**METHYLENE CHLORIDE** ($CH_2Cl_2$); a clear colorless liquid; standard 500 ppm). Used to remove caffeine from coffee, as the gas in aerosol cans, and as a solvent, degreaser, and paint remover. In May 1985 a Congressional survey found that 8.2 million pounds were emitted into the air every year from chemical plants around the country. Laboratory tests show that it can cause liver and lung cancer in mice. Local exposure to humans results in dry, scaly dermatitis, irritation to the eyes and upper respiratory tract, and skin burns. Systemic exposure affects the central nervous system, causing headaches, giddiness, irritability, numbness, and tingling in the limbs. In more serious cases there is anesthesia, hallucinations, pulmonary edema, coma, and in extreme instances, death from respiratory failure. Inconclusive evidence points to a possible link to cancer.

**METHYL CHLOROFORM. See 1,1,1-TRICHLOROETHANE.**

**METHYL ETHYL KETONE** ($C_4H_8O$; a clear flammable liquid; standard 200 ppm). Principally used in the synthetic rubber and drug industries. Over 3 million workers are exposed to this material on the job. It attacks the central nervous system and the lungs, resulting in irritation of the eyes and nose, headaches, dizziness, and vomiting. Also called butanone.

**METHYL IODIDE** (CH$_3$I; a colorless flammable liquid; standard 5 ppm). Used in the manufacture of many drugs and some pesticides. A known carcinogen in animals, methyl iodide can seriously damage the nervous system and cause fatal effects in humans from overexposure. Poisoning causes nausea, vertigo, slurred speech, drowsiness, dermatitis, skin blisters, and eye irritations. Also called iodomethane.

**METHYL ISOBUTYL KETONE** (C$_6$H$_{12}$O; a flammable liquid; standard 100 ppm). Used as a solvent for cellulose, gums, resins, fats, waxes, and oils. In foods, it is used as a synthetic fruit flavoring agent. Similar in toxicity to methyl ethyl ketone, it is irritating to eyes and mucous membranes. Intestinal upsets and central nervous system depression can also result from overexposure. Also called hexone.

**METHYL ISOCYANATE (MIC)** (C$_2$H$_3$NO; a highly flammable gas; standard 0.02 ppm). Used in the manufacture of insecticides. The first effect of exposure is watering of the eyes and damage to the corneas, making them opaque. When inhaled, MIC immediately constricts the passages of the nose, lungs, and larynx. The victim gasps for breath, as though suffering a severe asthma attack. The spasms are believed to be the result of MIC action on the nerve endings in the respiratory tract. If enough MIC is inhaled, sudden death results.

MIC can also irritate and inflame the lungs, leading to fluid accumulation. Breathing is both difficult and painful. Individuals who inhale enough MIC literally drown in their own secretions. Long-term effects of exposure include permanent damage to the liver, kidneys, and eyes, and a greater tendency to emphysema, asthma, and chronic bronchitis. The substance does not remain in the environment like dioxin, PCBs, or other noxious substances. Moisture in the air breaks down MIC. That is why, not long after the disaster at Bhopal, survivors were able to move back into their homes and drink the water.

Union Carbide's factory in Institute, West Virginia, is said to be the only producer of methyl isocyanate in the United States. The chemical is also manufactured in Japan, West Germany, Israel, South Korea, and Taiwan. See also **BHOPAL, INDIA, CHEMICALS.**

**METHYL PARATHION** ($C_8H_{10}NO_5PS$; a crystalline solid; standard 0.2 mg/m$^3$). An organic phosphorus compound that is finding increasing use as an insecticide. About 150,000 people are exposed to this substance through manufacture or use. It affects the body's enzymes. Among the symptoms of exposure are nausea and vomiting, abdominal cramps, diarrhea, involuntary defecation and urination, blurred vision, twitching, and breathing difficulty.

**METHYL PROPYL KETONE. See 2-PENTANONE.**

**METHYL SALICYLATE** ($C_8H_8O_3$ ; a colorless to reddish oily liquid). Used chiefly in perfumery and flavoring, and in medicine as a counterirritant in external preparations. Ingestion of relatively small amounts may cause severe poisoning and death. The first symptoms are nausea, vomiting, and pulmonary edema. Salicylates also interact unfavorably with a number of drugs, such as certain anticoagulants, antidepressants, and drugs for cancer and arthritis. Also called oil of wintergreen.

**MEVINPHOS** ($C_7H_{13}O_6P$; an orange liquid; standard 0.1 mg/m$^3$). Used mostly as an insecticide. It is dangerous to makers as well as users. In mild doses it causes runny nose, headache, wheezing, throat spasms, salivation, anorexia, nausea, abdominal cramps, and diarrhea. Higher amounts are responsible for low blood pressure, paralysis, and convulsions.

**MIC.** See **METHYL ISOCYANATE.**

**MICA** ($H_4 K_2 Al_6 Si_6 O_{24}$ ; colorless odorless flakes or sheets; standard 560,000 particles/m$^3$). Used in electrical equipment insulation and in the manufacture of roof shingles, wallpaper, and paint. Mica dust causes skin irritation on contact. When it is inhaled it attacks the lungs and coughing, weakness, and weight loss result. Also called muscovite.

**4-MMPD.** See **HAIR DYES.**

**MONOSODIUM GLUTAMATE (MSG)** ($C_5 H_9 NO_4$ ; a white crystalline powder). Used to intensify the flavor of foods. In 1908, Dr. Kikunae Ikeda, of Tokyo University, discovered that MSG made stronger the flavorings in meats, fish, poultry, seafood, cheese, and other foods containing proteins. In 1968, Ho Man Kwok discovered that MSG is responsible for the Chinese Restaurant Syndrome (CRS), in which some diners suffer a burning sensation in the back of the neck and forearms, chest tightness, and headaches about a half hour after eating a Chinese meal. In 1969 Dr. John Olney, of Washington University School of Medicine, St. Louis, Missouri, found that MSG destroyed nerve cells in the hypothalamus of certain animals. In October 1969 MSG was removed from baby food products.

# N

**NALED** ($C_4H_7Br_2Cl_2O_4P$; a colorless liquid; standard 3 mg/m$^3$). An insecticide that is dangerous both to makers and users. It causes many symptoms, from minor eye irritation, cramps, and weakness to paralysis, convulsions, and low blood pressure.

**NAPHTHA** ($C_{29}H_{32}O_{13}$; a colorless flammable liquid; standard 400 ppm). Used as a solvent in dry cleaning, and to make insecticides, rubber, paint, varnish, and plastics. It is made from petroleum or coal tar. Mildly injurious effects on users include skin chapping or burning and irritation of the eyes and upper respiratory tract; more severe is central nervous system depression, which can lead to dizziness, convulsions, and loss of consciousness.

**NAPHTHALENE** ($C_{10}H_8$; a white crystalline solid; standard 10 ppm). Usually prepared from coal tar, naphthalene is used mostly in making moth balls, dyes, and disinfectants. About 100 million people in the world have an enzyme deficiency that results in anemia if they are exposed to this substance. Of the total American population, about 0.1 percent suffer this deficiency. Among U.S. blacks, though, 20 percent are susceptible, and among Jews, 50 percent are susceptible. The continued inhalation of the dust or vapor of naphthalene, even without the enzyme deficiency, can cause such toxic symptoms as dermatitis, eye irritation, and cataracts. If a high concentration of the chemical gets into the system it can cause headaches, confusion, sweating, nausea and vomiting, abdominal pain, and bladder irritation. Possible long-term results are jaundice and kidney damage.

**NAPHTHENES.** A class of hydrocarbons with physical and chemical  properties similar to alkanes. Naphthenes are found in both crude oils and refined petroleum products. At low concentrations, the naphthenes can act as anesthetics; at high concentrations they attack the nervous system and may even lead to death.

**2-NAPHTHYLAMINE** ($C_{10}H_9N$; white crystals). Used mostly in the dye, rubber tire, chemical, coal gas, nickel, and copper industries. Having been found to cause bladder and pancreatic cancer, this material is now only used in research.

**NICKEL** (Ni; a metallic element; standard 1 mg/m$^3$). Applications found in shipbuilding, aerospace, and other heavy industries as well as for various electroplating, chemical, welding, and catalyst uses. Nickel is also part of ceramics, dyes, paints, and magnets. An estimated 1 million American workers are exposed to nickel; hundreds of thousands more people are in contact with the material because they live within a few miles of nickel plants. The EPA says that the entire population is exposed to low levels of nickel in the air, food, and water. Nickel causes various conditions ranging from "nickel itch," an eye and upper respiratory system irritation, to potential cancer of the nasal sinuses and the lungs. Research indicates that nickel can cause cancer in rats and guinea pigs. It also affects the reproduction of sea creatures. In humans it attacks the heart, brain, liver, and kidneys.

**NICOTINE** ($C_{10}H_{14}N_2$; a colorless odorless flammable oil with a sharp taste; standard 0.5 mg/m$^3$). A poison contained in the leaves of tobacco. Smokers, users of smokeless tobacco, and workers who handle tobacco are at greatest risk. There is some controversy about whether "passive smokers," nonsmokers in the same room with smokers, are also affected. Small doses of nicotine, as from smoking cigarettes, cigars, or pipes, can produce giddiness, nausea, and headache. Larger doses may lead to cold clammy sweats, vomiting, diarrhea, and collapse. If a considerable amount of nicotine enters the body, death may occur within three minutes.

**NITER.** See **POTASSIUM NITRATE.**

**NITRIC ACID** ($HNO_3$; a colorless liquid; standard 2 ppm). The second most important industrial acid; it is the sixth largest chemical industry in the United States. Nitric acid is mostly used in the production of fertilizers and explosives. The very toxic liquid is highly corrosive (eats into skin, metal, and other substances), gives off poisonous fumes, and is dangerously reactive (may cause fires or explosions). Intense pain and severe burns of skin result from contact; also, pulmonary disease from inhalation. Exposure to this material causes an accelerated respiratory rate, decreased vital capacity, low blood pressure, and an elevated blood platelet count. Nitric acid is an important ingredient of acid rain. Also called aqua fortis or azotic acid. See also **ACID RAIN.**

**NITRIC OXIDE** (NO; a colorless gas with a sharp, sweet odor; standard 25 ppm). Used to make nitric acid and in the production of certain plastics, paints, lacquers, and artificial fabrics. It is also encountered in blasting, welding, electroplating, and metal cleaning. The substance may be a hazard in case of fire in automobiles, power plants, or other buildings where it has been used. Nitric oxide also attacks the respiratory system and the lungs, causing irritation of the eyes, nose, and throat.

In high concentrations there may also be drowsiness and loss of consciousness. Also called nitrogen monoxide.

**NITRITES.** Salts or esters of nitrous acid. Used since prehistoric times as preservatives, they are currently added to bacon, hot dogs, and cold cuts to prevent spoilage and to give these products an attractive red color. Nitrites also add texture to rubber and plastic products such as infant pacifiers. In the 1970s government tests confirmed that, in the body, nitrites synthesized nitrosamines, many of which are carcinogenic. In 1978 the Agriculture Department ordered a reduction of nitrites added to cured meats to a maximum of 40 ppm. In January 1984 the CPSC limited nitrites in infant pacifiers and nipples to 60 ppb.

**NITROBENZENE** ($C_6 H_5 NO_2$; a pale-yellow flammable oily liquid with an odor of bitter almonds; standard 1 ppm). A highly toxic material, it is used in the manufacture of explosives and dyes, and is found in shoe polish, leather dressing, and paint solvent as well as several deodorizing products. The substance is dangerous when absorbed through the skin, swallowed, or inhaled as a vapor. It is especially dangerous to pregnant women, to those having a certain enzyme deficiency, and to those who drink alcohol. When toxic quantities of nitrobenzene are absorbed, the patient shows a bluish tinge in the fingernail beds, lips, ear lobes, mucous membranes, and tongue. The substance attacks the central nervous system, causing fatigue, headache, vertigo, weakness, depression, and even unconsciousness and coma. In acute form it damages the spleen, liver, and kidney. Also called oil of mirbane.

**NITROGEN DIOXIDES** ($NO_2$, $N_2 O_3$, and $N_2 O_4$; standard 5 ppm). Used in making nitric and sulfuric acid, and in liquid rocket fuel. Nitrogen dioxide is a major air pollutant; it also contributes to the oxidants in smog. About half the emissions are from vehicles; most of the rest are from power plants. Limited exposure can irritate the lungs, skin, eyes, and mucous membranes. High-level exposure can contribute to lowered resistance to respiratory infections and cause coughs, chills, headaches, nausea, vomiting, collapse, and in the worst cases, death. Even when the victim recovers, there may be permanent lung damage. The EPA reports that nitrogen dioxide levels nationwide have been going up in recent years. Strict federal standards for nitrogen dioxide emission from motor vehicles have not yet been enacted.

**NITROGEN MONOXIDE.** See **NITRIC OXIDE.**

**NITROPHENOLS.** Compounds made up of nitrogen, carbon, hydrogen, and oxygen. Nitrophenols are used in the manufacture of dyes and pesticides. In animal experiments the nitrophenols depress the central nervous system and result in labored breathing.

**NITROPROPANES.** A group of compounds containing nitrogen, carbon, hydrogen, and oxygen. Used in the manufacture of chemicals, as an ingredient in rocket and automobile fuels, and as a paint remover. Over 100,000 people are exposed to nitropropanes. Many others are exposed to the nitropropanes produced in tobacco smoke. In small doses they cause eye irritations, headache, nausea and vomiting, and diarrhea. Large doses are responsible for lung, liver, and kidney damage and loss of appetite. They are also suspected of being carcinogenic.

**NITROSAMINES.** A group of compounds that are suspected of being carcinogenic. See also **NITRITES, N-NITROSODIMETHYLAMINE,** and **SODIUM NITRATE.**

**N-NITROSODIMETHYLAMINE** ($C_2H_6N_2O$; a yellow liquid; no amount is safe). Used as an industrial solvent, gasoline additive, antioxidant, pesticide, in· rocket fuels, and in many industrial processes. It is a highly toxic and carcinogenic nitrosamine. Within a few hours after exposure, the victim suffers nausea and vomiting, abdominal cramps, diarrhea, headache, fever, and weakness. Liver damage can possibly result in death. The substance is linked to lung, liver, and kidney cancer in rats, guinea pigs, and other laboratory animals.

**NOISE** (standard 90 decibels). Loud, harsh, or confused sounds. Particularly affected are those who spend time in noisy workplaces and those who listen to music at too loud a volume. The result can be headaches and, in time, a permanent hearing loss. (44)

**NUTRASWEET.** See **ASPARTAME.**

# O

**OCTANE** ($C_8H_{18}$; a colorless flammable liquid with an odor like gasoline; standard 500 ppm). Used as a solvent and a fuel. An estimated 300,000 people are exposed to dangerous levels of octane. In high concentrations, affected individuals suffer irritation of the eyes and nose as well as drowsiness, dermatitis, and possibly pneumonia.

**OIL OF MIRBANE. See NITROBENZENE.**

**OIL OF WINTERGREEN. See METHYL SALICYLATE.**

**ORGANIC PHOSPHATES.** A group of chemicals that contain phosphorus and are used to control insects. Malathion, parathion, and leptophos are some better-known examples. Generally, these chemicals are short-lived, but some can be toxic when first applied. Acute symptoms may be as serious as paralysis, tremors, convulsions, and coma. Less serious are the drowsiness, confusion, cramps, sweating, and difficulty in breathing that may result.(11)

**OXIRANE. See ETHYLENE OXIDE.**

**OZONE** ($O_3$; a colorless gas with a pungent odor; standard 0.2 mg/m$^3$). Used as a food and water disinfectant, for bleaching textiles and paper pulp, for aging liquor and wood, and to dry varnishes and printing inks. It is formed in nature by the sun's action on the hydrocarbons and nitrogen oxides in the air from burning fuels, by electrical storms, and by X-ray machines, mercury vapor lamps, and electrical arcs.

Ozone is one of the most widespread of all air pollutants. It is the principal component of smog. According to researchers at North Carolina State University, almost 10 percent of the United States corn, wheat, soybean, and peanut crops are destroyed by ozone in the atmosphere. In Sequoia National Park, one-third of the ponderosa pine and black oak trees were damaged by ozone. Animal studies show that ozone increases the susceptibility to infection and leads to changes in cell membranes and lung tissue that can be fatal. In humans, ozone impairs breathing and severely irritates the mucous membranes of the nose and throat. The symptoms that arise from the presence of ozone are choking, coughs, sore throats, and extreme fatigue and chest discomfort.

# P

**PAHs.** See **POLYCYCLIC AROMATIC HYDROCARBONS.**

**PARAFFIN.** A white translucent mixture of hydrocarbons that is obtained from petroleum. Mild exposure causes chronic dermatitis and boils. Extreme exposure is linked to cancer of the scrotum.

**PARAQUAT** ($C_{12}H_{14}N_2Cl_2$; colorless cystals; standard 0.5 mg/m$^3$). Used as a pesticide, paraquat is an acutely toxic substance that the EPA has agreed to study. The first symptoms of exposure are burning of the mouth and throat, nausea and vomiting, and respiratory difficulty. Long-term, this substance can cause skin irritation, nosebleeds, and severe eye injury. A large dose is lethal.

**PARATHION** ($C_{10}H_{14}NO_5PS$; a pale-yellow liquid; standard 0.1 mg/m$^3$). An organic phosphorus compound used mostly as an insecticide. Parathion may be absorbed into the body in toxic amounts either through the skin or by inhalation. Approximately a quarter million workers are exposed in its manufacture and application. Once in the system, parathion inactivates an enzyme that plays an important role in the functioning of the nervous system, with sometimes fatal results. Severe intoxications have been reported from factories where it is handled in concentrated form, and from fields where it is mixed and applied for agricultural purposes. Among the many symptoms of parathion poisoning are headaches, wheezing, excessive salivation, nausea and vomiting, abdominal cramps, diarrhea, sweating, and weakness. In severe cases this is followed by lowered blood pressure, paralysis, convulsions, and death.

Of 30 farmworkers picking oranges in Riverside, California, in a grove that had been sprayed with parathion two and a half weeks earlier, 11 fell violently ill. Six hundred Mexican children ate pastries made with sugar that was contaminated with parathion; 17 died. The state of California reported 550 cases of parathion poisoning from 1969 through 1975, mostly among workers harvesting fruit.

**PBBs.** See **POLYBROMINATED BIPHENYLS.**

**PCBs.** See **POLYCHLORINATED BIPHENYLS.**

**PCNB.** See **PENTACHLORONITROBENZENE.**

**PCP.** See **PENTACHLOROPHENOL.**

**PENTACHLORONITROBENZENE (PCNB)** ($C_6 Cl_5 NO_2$ ; colorless needles; no federal standard). Used as a pesticide, soil fungicide, and in seed treatment. This substance has been found to cause cancer in two strains of mice. In September 1984 the EPA agreed to undertake a study of this chemical.

**PENTACHLOROPHENOL (PCP)** ($C_6 HCl_5 O$; a light-brown solid; standard 0.5 mg/m$^3$). A chlorinated hydrocarbon, it is used to protect wood against bacteria, fungi, and slime. It is also part of some general herbicides and insecticides, and appears as an ingredient in shampoos, paints, and laundry starches. In addition, the substance is found in bread, rice, candy, cereal, soft drinks, powdered milk, noodles, sugar, wheat, and water, either because the food had been sprayed with PCP or stored in containers treated with the chemical.

PCP is toxic when ingested, inhaled in the form of dust, or absorbed through the skin from solutions. The most generally noted symptoms are dermatitis, eye, nose, and throat irritation, anorexia and weight loss, chest pain, sweating, dizziness, fever, and difficulty in breathing. In large enough quantities, PCP can kill. In 1969 a hospital in St. Louis used an antibacterial soap that contained PCP. Nine infants washed with the soap fell ill; all needed intensive care, and two died. In Michigan in 1976 and 1977, 400 head of cattle fell ill after licking or breathing fumes from fences made with wood treated with PCP. Of 67 calves born, 61 were stillborn. See also **PHENOL** and **WOOD PRESERVATIVES.**

**2-PENTANONE** ($C_5H_{10}O$; a clear flammable liquid with a strong odor; standard 200 ppm). Used as a solvent and as a synthetic food flavoring. People exposed to this substance complain of marked irritation to the eyes and nasal passages. At greater concentrations this material is known to produce narcosis, coma, and death. Also known as methyl propyl ketone.

**PEPPERMINT CAMPHOR. See MENTHOL.**

**PERCHLOROBENZENE. See HEXACHLOROBENZENE.**

**PERCHLOROMETHANE. See CARBON TETRACHLORIDE.**

**PERCHLORYL FLUORIDE** ($ClFO_3$; a colorless gas with a sweet odor; standard 3 ppm). Used in the manufacture of rocket propellants and other chemicals. It is also found as an insulating gas in high-voltage electrical systems. People exposed to this gas suffer respiratory irritation and skin burns. Tests on animals show blood cell damage.

**PHENOL** ($C_6H_6O$; a white crystalline solid with an acrid odor; standard 5 ppm). Widely used in the manufacture of explosives, fertilizer, paint, rubber, textiles, drugs, and perfumes. The substance also finds use as a disinfectant in the petroleum, leather, paper, soap, and dye industries. Not only are the 10,000 workers in these industries at risk but also chemists, druggists, and biomedical personnel. Phenol vapors are flammable and can be quite dangerous in a fire. The chemical is very corrosive; it can damage the eyes or cause blindness, and can whiten and burn the skin. Absorption into the body can occur through the gastrointestinal tract or through the lungs. After absorption, the toxicity affects the central nervous system, leading to paleness, weakness, sweating, headache, and frothing at the nose and mouth. After sufficient exposure there can also be damage to the lungs, kidneys, liver, pancreas, and spleen. Severe cases usually result in death within a few hours. The material has been found to be toxic to fish. Also called carbolic acid. See also **PENTACHLOROPHENOL** and **WOOD PRESERVATIVES.**

**PHENOTHIAZINE** ($C_{12}H_9NS$; greenish crystalline solid; no federal standard). Used as a drug to get rid of intestinal worms in humans and animals. It is also employed in drug manufacture. This substance may irritate the skin on contact, turn hair and nails reddish-brown, and cause abdominal cramps. It may also damage the kidneys and lead to such conditions as hepatitis, anemia, and conjunctivitis.

**N-PHENYL-BETA-NAPHTHYLAMINE** ($C_{16}H_{13}N$; a light-gray powder; no federal standard). Used in the manufacture of rubber and lubricants. It is linked to bladder cancer.

**PHOSGENE** ($CCl_2O$; a colorless gas with a sweet odor; standard 0.1 ppm). Used in the manufacture of dyes, metal products, insecticides, and drugs. This toxic chemical was used as a poison gas in World War I. Its inhalation affects the throat, eyes, and lungs. Since the least detectable odor is 5.6 ppm, it is possible to inhale phosgene with no warning symptoms for an hour or so. Chronic exposure leads to pulmonary edema, dizziness, chills, coughing, and a choking sensation. It can also cause emphysema and pneumonia. Death from respiratory or cardiac failure can result from acute overexposure. Also called carbon oxychloride and carbonyl chloride.

**PHOSPHINE** ($PH_3$; a colorless flammable gas with the odor of decaying fish; standard 0.4 mg/m$^3$). Although rarely used, it arises as a by-product in various industrial processes, such as rust-proofing or metal-shaving. It also is generated during grain fumigation by aluminum phosphide or calcium phosphide. The substance burns very easily and is therefore a dangerous fire and explosion hazard. Inhalation affects the eyes and causes dilation of the pupils. A high concentration in the air is rapidly fatal, producing fainting, lowered blood pressure, paralysis, and coma. Although it has a nauseating odor, it is barely noticeable at 20 times the maximum allowable amount. Also called hydrogen phosphide.

**PHOSPHORIC ACID** ($H_3PO_4$; a colorless liquid; standard 1 mg/m$^3$). Used in the manufacture of fertilizers, detergents, animal feed, dental cement, drugs, soft drinks, and gelatine and in other industries (engraving, lithography, metal cleaning, sugar refining). This highly toxic and corrosive liquid is very dangerous to the eyes and skin. Under certain conditions it can be responsible for respiratory difficulties, especially when dispersed in the air as a mist.

**PHOSPHORUS** (P; flammable solid element; standard 0.1 mg/m$^3$). Used to make ammunition, fireworks, explosives, and smoke bombs. A toxic chemical, phosphorus ignites spontaneously when exposed to air. Contact with the skin results in severe burns. High concentrations of the vapors from burning phosphorus are irritating to the skin, eyes, nose, throat, and lungs. The absorption of toxic quantities of phosphorus through the lungs or gastrointestinal tract has an acute effect on the liver, and is accompanied by vomiting and marked weakness. Long-term absorption of small amounts of phosphorus can result in necrosis of the jaw bone, a condition known as "phossy-jaw." It can also cause changes in the body's bones, making them brittle and leading to spontaneous fractures. As a nutrient, phosphorus is essential to aquatic life in small amounts. At higher levels it can stimulate the growth of algae and seaweed. This tends to speed up eutrophication (the aging of lakes and reservoirs) and use up the water's dissolved oxygen.

**PHTHALATES.** A family of chemicals used to make soft plastics, such as furniture covers, for example. A known carcinogen in mice, phthalates are now under study for their toxic effects in humans. Repeated exposure to even low concentrations of these fumes is irritating to eyes, skin, and respiratory tract. Chronic exposure causes bronchitis, emphysema, asthma, and permanent eye damage.

**PICLORAM** ($C_6 H_3 Cl_3 N_2 O_2$ ; a colorless powder with chlorine odor; no federal standard). Used as an herbicide to get rid of brush. It is a suspected carcinogen for workers and users.

**PLUTONIUM.** A synthetic radioactive element that is formed in nuclear reactors. See also **RADIOACTIVE SUBSTANCES.**

**POLYBROMINATED BIPHENYLS (PBBs).** A group of compounds containing bromine that are used as fire retardants. These substances are found in plastics that are made heat resistant, such as those used in typewriters, calculators, and business machines as well as in radio and TV parts, hand tools, and electrical equipment. No human effects are currently known, but many fear that some diseases may appear in time since in laboratory studies, PBBs are known to attack the liver, kidney, and skin of animals.

In 1973 about two tons of PBBs were accidentally mixed with animal feed and given to cattle in Michigan. The cattle showed weight loss, reduced milk, and damage to fetuses. Two hundred and fifty dairy farms and 500 cattle farms were quarantined. As a precaution, 30,000 cattle and swine were killed, but only after many had been slaughtered and sold. (11)

**POLYCHLORINATED BIPHENYLS (PCBs)** (colorless liquids, nonflammable; standard $0.001$ mg/m$^3$). A group of about 200 compounds containing chlorine, carbon, and hydrogen. They are oily, synthetic substances. Because the PCBs are fire resistant they are used in electrical equipment manufacture as insulators and as coolants. They were also used as lubricants and plasticizers. This family of toxic compounds, first manufactured in 1930, is usually referred to in the plural since it always includes several closely related chemicals.

PCBs are picked up by the body's cells because they resemble needed chemicals. They then tend to accumulate and remain in the tissue. It is believed that the PCBs may cause liver damage, birth defects, and severe acne in humans. In Japan, children born to mothers who were exposed to excessive PCBs were retarded and clumsy. And children living near Lake Michigan who ate local trout with high levels of PCBs developed many behavioral problems. Animal experiments show that they can cause cancer and are also linked to a low birth rate. PCBs are responsible for eggshell thinning in birds, and are suspected in reproductive failure in fish.

Epidemiological studies at two General Electric plants in New York State that used large amounts of PCBs have contributed to the understanding of the dangers of these chemicals. In the early 1970s some 65 workers became ill with asthmatic bronchitits, dizziness, nose and eye irritations, nausea, dermatitis, and acne. A 1976 survey found that 45 percent of the workers had skin problems of one kind or another, and 40 percent were suffering with various types of eye or ear complaints. During this period, the two plants dumped about 1.5 million pounds of PCBs into the Hudson River. In Poughkeepsie, New York, a city on the Hudson that draws its drinking water from the river, the number of cases of colon and rectal cancer was far above average. A bass caught in the river had 340 ppm of PCBs, which is 70 times above the allowable level in food. The record was an eel whose tissue contained 559 ppm—over half of the total lifetime safety limit for a human.

Over the years, the government has been taking steps to restrict the amount of PCBs in the environment. Pesticides containing PCBs were banned in 1970. In 1973 standards on the level of PCBs in foods and the amounts that could be discharged into rivers or lakes was set . Finally, in 1979 the EPA banned all manufacturing, processing, and distribution of PCBs. Yet, despite all these actions, traces of PCBs can still be found in the soil, water, and air as well as in fish, animal, and human tissue. (11)

**POLYCYCLIC AROMATIC HYDROCARBONS (PAHs).** A group of organic compounds produced by the burning of fuels. The major sources are power plants, incinerators, and coke ovens. Cars and trucks produce about 1 percent of the PAHs overall, but as much as 50 percent in the cities. Rubber and tire manufacturers also use processing oils that contain PAHs. The PAHs include such known carcinogens as anthracene and the suspected cancer-causing agent naphthalene. Animals tested with PAHs get cancer of the stomach, lung, breast, or skin.

**POLYVINYL CHLORIDE (PVC).** Polyvinyl chloride is a term that is loosely applied to a large number of vinyl chloride polymers that are widely used for many different purposes. Among the more important applications are to make phonograph records and floor covering and as an insulator for metal pipes and wire. The major hazard of PVC is that it releases hydrochloric acid when burned. See also **VINYL CHLORIDE.**

**POTASSIUM BROMATE** ($KBrO_3$ ; a white crystalline powder). Used chiefly as an oxidizing agent and a bread improver. Although the lethal dose for humans has not been determined, at high concentrations serious cases of poisoning have been reported, including central nervous system problems and death apparently due to kidney failure. It is also a dangerous fire and explosion hazard.

**POTASSIUM HYDROXIDE** (KOH; a white solid usually in the form of lumps, sticks, or pellets). Used chiefly in the manufacture of soap, as a laboratory reagent, and in medicine as a caustic. Food manufacturers also use it to remove the skins of various fruits. It is an extremely corrosive material and very dangerous to eyes and skin. Inhalation of the fumes is very dangerous to the respiratory tract, but since the material is a solid, this normally is not a problem. Ingestion may produce violent pain in the stomach, bleeding, and collapse. The FDA banned household products containing more than 10 percent potassium hydroxide. Also called caustic potash.

**POTASSIUM NITRATE** ($KNO_3$ ; a colorless or white crystalline powder with a salty taste). Used in gunpowder, fireworks, fertilizers, and preservatives. Potassium nitrate is used as a color fixative in cured meat products (up to .02 percent), in pickling brine (7 pounds per 100 gallons), and in chopped meat (2.75 ounces per 100 pounds). The FDA is testing potassium nitrate for possible cancer-causing, mutagenic, and reproductive effects. Also known as saltpeter and niter.

**POTASSIUM NITRITE** ($KNO_2$ ; white to yellowish needles). Used as a color fixative in cured meats (up to .02 percent) and as an oxidizing agent. The substance is a dangerous fire and explosion hazard. In the body nitrite combines with natural stomach and food chemicals to form the powerful cancer-causing agents nitrosamines and nitrosamides. The law limits the residue on ready-to-eat meat to 200 ppm. The FDA is testing potassium nitrite for cancer-causing, mutagenic, and reproductive effects.

**POTASSIUM SULFATE** ($K_2 SO_4$ ; white crystals). Used chiefly in the manufacture of fertilizers, alums, and mineral water and as a reagent in analytical chemistry. It is also a water corrective used in the brewing industry. Large doses can attack the gastrointestinal tract and cause severe bleeding.

**PROPANONE.** See **ACETONE.**

**PROPENE NITRILE.** See **ACRYLONITRILE.**

**PROPYLENE OXIDE** ($C_3 H_6 O$; a colorless, flammable liquid with an etherlike odor; standard 100 ppm). An ingredient in brake fluid that is also used in the manufacture of detergents and other products. It can irritate the eyes and cause damage to lungs and skin. In animal experiments, the substance is carcinogenic.

**PRUSSIC ACID.** See **HYDROGEN CYANIDE.**

**PVC.** See **POLYVINYL CHLORIDE.**

**PYRIDINE** ($C_5 H_5 N$; a colorless flammable liquid with a sharp odor; standard 5 ppm). Usually obtained from coal or synthesized from acetaldehyde and ammonia, and used chiefly as a solvent and in organic synthesis. Food manufacturers use pyridine in chocolate flavorings for beverages, ice cream, ices, candy, and baked goods. When large quantities are inhaled or ingested, the substance is absorbed from the respiratory or gastrointestinal tract and can cause headaches, vertigo, and trembling. It is an irritant to eyes and mucous membranes and produces narcotic effects by attacking the central nervous system.

# Q

**QUICKLIME.** See **CALCIUM OXIDE.**

**QUINONE** ($C_6H_4O_2$ ; large yellow crystals; standard 0.1 ppm). Used in the dye and cosmetic industries. Quinone is an irritant material that is particularly dangerous to the eyes, and even brief exposure to high concentrations of the vapor can cause dangerous disturbances of vision. Contact with the skin can result in skin discoloration and damage. Prolonged exposure may lead to swelling and ulceration. Also called chinone.

# R

**RADIOACTIVE SUBSTANCES.** Harmful particles and rays that come from natural sources (cosmic rays and the uranium, thorium, and radium found in the earth), from human activities (such as X-rays, nuclear reactors, nuclear-weapon tests, and color TV), and from radioactive wastes. When radiation strikes the body, it gives electrical charges to the cells. These charges change the cells and can cause cancer or reproductive damage. They can also kill cells. If a massive number of cells are killed, death results.

Chiefly at risk from radioactive substances are uranium miners, radiologists, and workers in the nuclear industry. But X-rays, color TV, the danger of a nuclear accident, and radioactive wastes put everyone in some danger.

There are three types of radioactive waste: *High-level* radioactive wastes are generated in the reprocessing of radioactive fuel after it has been used in a nuclear reactor. *Transuranic* waste comes from the reprocessing and fabrication of plutonium to make nuclear weapons. And *low-level* wastes are derived from the solutions as well as the rags, clothes, and tools used for cleaning and decontaminating nuclear reactors. Most waste must be stored securely for at least 10,000 years. For example, plutonium 239, the fuel of breeder reactors, remains highly hazardous for 24,000 years! See also **INDOOR POLLUTION, PLUTONIUM, RADIUM,** and **RADON.** (23)

**RADIUM** (Ra; a silver-white radioactive metallic element). Mostly used in treating cancer. The radium atoms are constantly giving off radiation made up of particles and rays. This radiation is extremely toxic and hazardous to human cells and causes different types of cancer. But it has also been found that the radiation does more damage to cancer cells than to healthy cells. Therefore it is used in treating certain types of cancer. Death can result from extreme exposure to radium. See also **RADIOACTIVE SUBSTANCES.**

**RADON** (Rn; a colorless odorless radioactive gas). A rare element given off by uranium and radium that is sometimes used in treating cancer. Radon itself, though, is known to be a cause of skin, lung, and bone cancer, and leukemia. The cancer, though, has a latency period of 10 to 15 years. At an international conference held in Sweden in 1984, the scientists concluded that up to 10 percent of all lung cancer is caused by radon. Radon is continuously seeping up out of the ground throughout the world. It comes particularly from granite and other rocks.

In February 1984 high concentrations of radon, some as much as 100 times above government safety levels, were found in a number of New Jersey homes. It was found that the radon is seeping up from uranium deposits in a rock formation, called the Reading Prong, which runs under parts of Pennsylvania, New Jersey, and New York. An estimated 100,000 homes are located above the Reading Prong. A survey of 2,500 of these homes showed that 40 percent had radon levels above the safety limit. Late in 1985 the EPA started a nationwide survey to find other areas with high radon levels and studies to determine the best ways to protect homes from the gas. See also **INDOOR POLLUTION** and **RADIOACTIVE SUBSTANCES.**

**RED 3, RED 40.** See **FOOD COLORS.**

**RESORCINOL** ($C_6 H_6 O_2$ ; white flammable crystals). Used in hair dyes, some drugs, and as an adhesive in various rubber products. In solution, this substance can readily be absorbed through the skin and can cause skin irritations and chronic health problems. It also acts both as a blood and nerve poison, causing restlessness, cyanosis, convulsions, and death. These same symptoms occur after ingestion of the substance. There is also some evidence that resorcinol is animal carcinogenic.

**RONNEL** ($C_8 H_8 Cl_{1\,3} O_3$ PS; tan waxy solid; standard 15 mg/m$^3$ ). Insecticide used in homes and farms. Ronnel is an eye irritant, but it also causes liver and kidney damage. Possibly linked to cancer, it has a risk of teratogenicity and is dangerous to a fetus.

**ROTENONE** ($C_{23} H_{22} O_6$ ; colorless to red solid; standard 5 mg/m$^3$ ). A known irritant, it is used primarily as an insecticide. The dust causes irritation of the lungs; in sensitive individuals it gives rise to allergic symptoms. Also affected are the eyes and skin. Tremors, convulsions, and stupor may result from exposure. A possible carcinogen, rotenone is regarded as a mutagen and teratogen.

# S

**SACCHARIN** ($C_7 H_5 NO_3 S$; a synthetically produced white powder). Used chiefly as a noncaloric sugar substitute in the manufacture of syrups, foods, and beverages. In dilute solution, saccharin is 300-500 times sweeter than sugar. Saccharin was discovered by accident in 1879, by Constanin Fahlberg, a chemist at Johns Hopkins University. At first it was used only by diabetics, who could not eat sugar. Since 1960 it has been used as a "diet" sweetener in soft drinks and sweeteners. Soft drinks contain 150 mg per serving. Paper packets of sweetener contain 20 to 50 mg (the equivalent of 1 to 2 teaspoons of sugar). Saccharin tests on laboratory animals at high dosages for extended time have produced kidney damage as well as bladder cancer and leukemia.

Saccharin was listed as a suspected animal carcinogen by the National Toxicology Project and the International Agency for Research on Cancer. The FDA is awaiting analysis of information from a seven-year congressional study on its mutagenic and reproductive effects. For now, the FDA has proposed limiting saccharin to one gram a day for a 150-pound person. Although still approved by the FDA the current label reads: "Use of this product may be hazardous to your health. This product contains saccharin which has been determined to cause cancer in laboratory animals."

**SAL SODA.** See **SODIUM CARBONATE.**

**SALTPETER.** See **POTASSIUM NITRATE.**

**SASSAFRAS.** An herb that is used in folk medicine as a muscle relaxant and as a treatment for rheumatism, skin disease, and typhus. It contains safrole, an oil that had once been used in root beer. Sassafras is a suspected carcinogen in mice and rats. The FDA has banned sassafras and safrole as flavors or additives. One cup of sassafras tea contains 200 mg of safrole, four times the amount that is considered hazardous.

**SILICA** ($SiO_2$ ; a crystalline solid; standard 5 mg/m$^3$). Used chiefly in the form of a white powder in the manufacture of fiberglass, ceramics, and abrasives. NIOSH says that 1.2 million workers are exposed to silica. Affected people suffer symptoms such as coughing, wheezing, and breathing difficulty. Chronic lung disease (silicosis), which is progressive and frequently incapacitating, is common among miners and workers in the glass and ceramics industries as well as among those who work in factories where the silica is used as an abrasive. Also called cristabolite.

**SMOKELESS TOBACCO.** As the dangers of smoking cigarettes become better known, more and more young people are using smokeless tobacco. The two kinds are snuff (shredded tobacco held between the gum and cheek) and chewing tobacco (a wad of tobacco held in the mouth). A study in Louisiana showed a six-fold increase in snuff use among boys of all ages. In Massachusetts, 28 percent of high school boys reported some experience with smokeless tobacco. The health hazards of smokeless tobacco range from mouth sores, gum disease, and tooth loss, to cancer of the mouth, pharynx, and esophagus. In some cases, the cancer results in death.

**SMOG.** A word compounded of *smoke* and *fog*. It is a mixture of various chemicals formed in the air from automotive emissions of hydrocarbons and nitrogen oxides. One of the most common compounds formed is ozone. See also **OZONE.**

**SNUFF.** See **SMOKELESS TOBACCO.**

**SODA ASH.** See **SODIUM CARBONATE.**

**SODIUM AZIDE** ($NaN_3$; a white crystalline solid; no federal standard). Widely used in manufacturing explosives, fungicides, nematocides, soil fumigants, and wines. Lumber dealers use sodium azide to prevent discoloring and beer makers use it to kill fungus. This substance is poisonous, much like cyanide salts. In small doses it lowers blood pressure, and it is even used as a drug for hypertension. Overdoses, though, lead to heart palpitations and loss of consciousness, followed by rapid recovery. It can, however, lead to respiratory arrest, convulsions, and heart failure. Found to be a mutagen in plants and bacteria, sodium azide is a suspected carcinogen. Furthermore, it is unstable and can explode when exposed to heat or great shock.

**SODIUM CARBONATE** ($Na_2CO_3$; white odorless crystals; no federal standard). Used in the manufacture of glass, ceramics, soaps, paper, petroleum, sodium salts, and in water treatment. In the food industry sodium carbonate is used as a neutralizer for butter, cream, milk, ice cream, in the processing of olives before canning, and in cocoa products. A strong alkali, as a dust it is very irritating to eyes and nose and the entire upper respiratory tract when inhaled. Ingestion of large doses may affect the gastrointestinal tract, causing vomiting, diarrhea, circulatory collapse, and even death. Also called soda ash or sal soda.

**SODIUM FLUOROACETATE** ($NaC_2H_2FO_2$; a fluffy colorless solid; standard 0.05 mg/m$^3$). Used mostly as a rat poison. The substance can cause vomiting, hallucinations, facial twitch, convulsions, and an irregular pulse in humans. More serious effects include heart disturbances and pulmonary edema.

**SODIUM NITRATE** (NaNO$_3$; colorless odorless flammable crystals; no federal standard). Used in fertilizers, explosives, and glass. Sodium nitrate is also a color fixative and taste-enhancer in cured meats, frankfurters, bacon, bologna, and other processed meats and fish as well as a preservative to prevent the growth of bacteria that cause botulism or food poisoning. Nitrates combine with natural stomach and food substances to form powerful carcinogens known as nitrosamines. Nitrosamines have been found in nitrate-treated fish. Overdoses cause death by cutting off oxygen from the brain. The FDA allows 500 ppm in food. Nitrates are being tested by the FDA for possible carcinogenic, mutagenic, and reproductive effects.

**SODIUM NITRITE** (NaNO$_2$; white to yellow flammable powder or needles; no federal standard). Used mostly to make meats such as bacon, bologna, and frankfurters redder in color; also used in bleaching and dyeing. Sodium nitrite resists the growth of botulism-causing bacteria. It is added to an estimated seven billion pounds of food each year. Deaths have resulted from ingesting sodium nitrite residue in food, such as meat tenderizer, which contains almost pure sodium nitrite. In certain forms, such as fried bacon, it is believed to be carcinogenic to humans. The government allows 200 ppm in food. Since 1976 it has not been allowed to be used in baby foods. The FDA is studying sodium nitrite for cancer-causing, mutagenic, and reproductive effects.

**SOLVENT FUMES.** Irritating gas or vapor from solvents. Solvents are widely used in industry, including the manufacture of computer chips. Two particular solvents, trichloroethane and methyl ketones, are known to affect the nervous system. A 1980 survey by the California Department of Industrial Relations found that 42 chip companies used one-half million gallons of solvents. Workers in this industry show such symptoms of solvent exposure as slow nerve conduction, impaired memory and concentration, and decreased sensation in fingertips. A number of solvents have been found to be carcinogenic in animals.

**SOOTS. See COKE-OVEN FUMES.**

**STACK GAS. See FLUE GAS.**

**STANNOUS CHLORIDE** ($SnCl_4$; a white crystalline solid; standard 2 mg/m$^3$). Used in the manufacture of dyes and to revive yeast. As an antioxidant it is used in processing soft drinks, canned asparagus, and other foods. Vapors may cause irritation to the skin and mucous membranes. The FDA is studying stannous chloride for possible mutagenic and reproductive effects. Also called fuming tin chloride.

**STIBINE** ($SbH_3$; a colorless flammable gas; standard 0.5 mg/m$^3$). Used in fumigating and in filling hydrogen balloons. The gas is produced when charging storage batteries, welding, soldering, etching, and during certain chemical processes. A powerful blood and central nervous system poison, this material can cause permanent blood changes and liver damage. Symptoms are nausea, weakness, abdominal pain, slow breathing, weak and irregular pulse, and even jaundice and death.

**STRYCHNINE** ($C_{21}H_{22}N_2O_2$; a colorless crystalline powder; standard 0.15 mg/m$^3$). Used mostly as a poison to kill rats, mice, and moles, this extremely toxic substance also attacks the central nervous system of humans. Its first symptoms are uneasiness and irritability. Convulsive movements and excruciating pain can follow, causing the patient to shriek in agony. Spasms of great violence may arch the body, with the affected person resting on head and feet, eyes staring, face livid, chest and abdomen stiff. Foaming at the mouth, asphyxia, and coma may result. Death sometimes follows, due to exhaustion and asphyxia.

**SULFITES.** Chemicals added to many wines, beers, and drugs, and applied to fruit, vegetables, and fish to keep them looking fresh. The sulfites can cause severe allergic reactions ranging from hives, nausea, and diarrhea to coma, brain damage, and death. About 5 percent of people with asthma are especially sensitive to the sulfites. It is believed that from 1982 to 1985 at least twelve people died as a result of ingesting sulfites.

**SULFUR DIOXIDE** ($SO_2$ ; a colorless gas with a strong suffocating odor like rotten eggs; standard 5 ppm). Formed primarily during the combustion of high-sulfur fossil fuels (coal and oil). About 80 percent of sulfur dioxide emissions result from the combustion of fossil fuels, principally by electric utilities. It is also synthesized and used in the manufacture of chemicals, such as sulfuric acid, in preserving fruits and vegetables, and in bleaching, disinfecting, and fumigating applications.

One of the major air pollutants, sulfur dioxide reacts in the atmosphere to form sulfates and related compounds that are seriously unhealthy for plants, animals, and people. It can, though, be removed by one of several cleaning techniques prior to the venting of the stack gases. Sulfates contribute to visibility problems and to acid rain. It is very irritating to mucous membranes of the upper respiratory tract. The first symptoms include cough, dry throat, and conjunctivitis. Corneal burns and opacity of the eyes occur after direct contact. Prolonged exposure may result in lung damage or death from asphyxia. When found with high amounts of particulates it is thought to cause an increase in the death rate, especially among those with heart and lung disease. Laboratory animals show a possible link between sulfur dioxide and cancer. See also **ACID RAIN.**

**SULFURIC ACID** ($H_2SO_4$; a colorless odorless oily liquid; standard 1 mg/m$^3$). Used in the manufacture of many chemicals as well as in fertilizers, explosives, artificial fibers, dyes, drugs, detergents, glue, paint, paper, furs, and food products. An estimated 200,000 workers in these industries are exposed to the corrosive effects of this material. Locally, there is charring of the skin, damage to the eyes, and burns in the mouth if swallowed. Long-term it eats away the teeth and results in chronic bronchitis with faster, more shallow breathing.

# T

**2,4,5-T.** See **2,4,5-TRICHLOROPHENOXYACETIC ACID.**

**TALC** ($H_2O_3SiMg_3$; a soft green-to-gray mineral; no federal standard). Used in making lubricants, talcum powder, and for electrical insulation. It is also found in vitamin supplements and in chewing gum. Inhalation of talc dust can cause lung irritation. Ingestion is suspected of causing stomach cancer among the Japanese who treat their rice with talc, since it has a chemical composition similar to asbestos, a known carcinogen.

**TCDD.** See **TETRACHLORODIOXIN.**

**TCE.** See **TRICHLOROETHYLENE.**

**TDI.** See **TOLUENE DIISOCYANATE.**

**TETRACHLORODIOXIN.** Considered by many scientists to be the most toxic chemical in the group of compounds known as dioxin. See also **DIOXIN.**

**1,1,2,2-TETRACHLOROETHANE** ($C_2H_2Cl_4$; a heavy sweet-smelling liquid; standard 5 ppm). Used in dry cleaning, as a fumigant, and in the manufacture of artificial silk and artificial pearls. About 11,000 workers are exposed to this chemical. Contact with the skin can result in scaly dermatitis. Prolonged and extensive exposure can cause tremors, headache, numbness, sweating, loss of reflexes, and even paralysis and blood disturbances. Even more serious is the eye or liver damage, jaundice, delirium, and convulsions that sufferers endure after absorption or inhalation.

**TETRAMETHYL THIURANE DISULFIDE.** See **THIRAM.**

**THIRAM** ($C_6 H_{12} N_2 S_4$; white or yellow crystals; standard 5 mg/m$^3$). Used to control bacteria in edible oils and fats, as an ingredient in suntan and antiseptic sprays and soaps, and as a seed, nut, fruit, and mushroom disinfectant. This material is a known irritant of mucous membranes, causing sneezing, coughing, and skin and eye irritations. Individuals get a particularly bad reaction if they drink alcohol while exposed to thiram. This reaction led to the development of a related compound called Antabuse that is now sold as a drug. Antabuse produces severely disagreeable symptoms after alcohol is drunk and is used to help break the drinking habit. Thiram is also known by its full name, tetramethyl thiurane disulfide.

**THM.** See **CHLOROFORM.**

**THORIUM** (Th; flammable metallic element). A natural radioactive element used in nuclear reactors and for some industrial processes. See also **RADIOACTIVE SUBSTANCES.**

**THORIUM OXIDE** ($ThO_2$; a white heavy powder; no federal standard). Used chiefly in the chemical, steel, ceramics, and incandescent lamp industries. It is also found around nuclear reactors and metal refineries. Exposed workers are at risk of cancer of the liver.

**TIMES BEACH, MISSOURI, CHEMICALS.** A one-mile-square town on the Meramec River, 25 miles west of St. Louis, that was contaminated by dioxin. In 1971, Russell Bliss, of Fenton, Missouri, collected 18,000 gallons of waste liquids from a chemical plant. On May 26 of that year he sprayed a mixture of these wastes and used motor oil that he had collected from service stations in the area in the stables of a horse farm near St. Louis to keep down the dust. Over the next weeks, hundreds of birds nesting in the rafters as well as numbers of rats and mice living in the stables fell dead. Over the following months a total of 48 out of the 125 horses in the stables also died. In 1974 the Centers for Disease Control discovered that the chemical plant wastes were laced with dioxin.

Before this finding was made, though, Mr. Bliss had sprayed the same mixture of waste chemicals and oil on the dirt roads of Times Beach to control the dust. In December 1982 flood waters spread the dioxin, and the EPA found 300 ppm of dioxin under the town's roads. The government considers anything above 1 ppb of dioxin as dangerous. The EPA eventually appropriated $33 million to buy all the houses and businesses of the 2,000 residents who wanted to leave the town. (3)

**TIN** (Sn; a metallic element; standard 2 mg/m$^3$). Used to plate other metals and to make alloys, tinfoil, and soft solders. The substance affects aluminum and steel workers, welders, solderers, miners, smelters, and refiners. The first symptoms are mild irritation to skin and mucous membranes. Prolonged exposure to the fumes or dust may result in pneumoconiosis, a respiratory disease.

**TNA.** See **TRINITROTOLUENE.**

**TNT.** See **TRINITROTOLUENE.**

**TOBACCO SMOKE.** A major indoor pollutant, tobacco contains more than 3,000 chemical components, including such carcinogens as arsenic, formaldehyde, nitrites, vinyl chloride, and several others. They are known to attack the lungs, liver, and esophagus. Tobacco smoke is found in many indoor living and work spaces, especially where the windows are sealed and stale air recirculates.

The carcinogenic effects of tobacco smoke were first noticed about 200 years ago. In 1950, the first major proof was produced, linking cigarette smoke with lung cancer. Today it is known to cause one-third of all cancer deaths. Since 1970 the label on a pack of cigarettes carries this message: "Warning: The Surgeon General has determined that cigarette smoking is dangerous to your health." Currently there are proposed congressional bills that would warn that smoking "is addictive" and is responsible for "death from" cancer, emphysema, heart disease, and an increased chance of miscarriage.

About three-fourths of the nicotine from cigarette smoking ends up in the atmosphere. So-called passive smokers can also inhale radioactive particles, called radon daughters, from the emissions of others' cigarettes. Passive tobacco smoke is believed by some experts to be the most dangerous airborne carcinogen. The EPA estimates that 500 to 5,000 nonsmokers die of lung cancer every year as a result of other people's cigarettes. In 1982 a total of 116,270 Americans died of lung cancer; close to 100,000 of these deaths were related to cigarette smoking. By comparison, coke-oven emissions, the second most dangerous airborne carcinogen, causes fewer than 150 lung cancer deaths per year. See also **NICOTINE** and **SMOKELESS TOBACCO.**


**2,4-TOLUENEDIAMINE** ($C_7H_{10}N_2$; colorless needles; no federal standard). Used to make dyes for the textile, leather, fur, silk, wood, paper, and cotton industries. Up until 1971 it was used in hair dyes. The substance produces black, dark-blue, and brown colors. It is an irritant for eyes and skin.

Nausea, vomiting, jaundice, and anemia as well as central nervous system and liver damage can result from exposure.

**TOLUENE DIISOCYANATE (TDI)** ($C_9 H_6 N_2 O_2$ ; a colorless or yellow liquid with sweet odor; standard 0.02 ppm). Obtained chiefly from coal tar and petroleum, TDI is mostly used to make polyurethane plastics. Affected are about 40,000 who work in small workplaces with polyurethane, adhesives, insulation, paint sprays, lacquers, rubber, and textiles. This material came into wide use in the 1950s. It irritates any living tissue it touches, especially the mucous membranes, eyes, and the respiratory tract. The vapor causes nausea, vomiting, abdominal pain, and breathing problems. It can also cause temporary headaches, insomnia, and paranoid depression. Exposure over weeks or years causes some people to become sensitized to TDI, altering the protein in lung tissues and leading to severe allergic reaction, with asthmatic attacks. According to NIOSH there are no safe concentrations of this substance. Anemia and blood cell damage are possible long-term effects. (50)

**TOXAPHENE** ($C_{10} H_{10} Cl_8$ ; an amber-colored waxy solid; standard 0.5 mg/m$^3$). Most widely used outdoor insecticide, particularly on crops, mainly cotton. Makers and users are at risk from the effects of this toxic substance. A known carcinogen in animals, it is suspected of causing cancer in humans as well. Among its other effects are nausea, confusion, agitation, tremors, convulsions, and unconsciousness. Toxaphene also causes genetic abnormalities in animals and kills wildlife. In December 1978 the California Department of Food and Agriculture treated 850 cattle with toxaphene to control parasites. Between 70 and 95 of the cows died. Five hundred later either aborted, or their calves soon died. A dog ate the flesh from one dead cow and also fell dead. Also called chlorinated camphene. (11)

**1,2,4-TRICHLOROBENZENE** ($C_6 H_3 Cl_3$ ; a colorless flammable solid or liquid with a pleasant aroma; no federal standard). Used mostly in dyes and herbicides. The greatest human exposure is through runoff water and drinking water. This substance is irritating to the respiratory system and the eyes and can damage the liver. Its effects can be serious. Skin contact with the compound or inhalation can cause skin, eye, and upper respiratory tract irritations. Excessive exposure brings on drowsiness, lack of coordination, and unconsciousness. In animals, experiments have found liver, kidney, and lung damage.

**1,1,1-TRICHLOROETHANE** ($C_2 H_3 Cl_3$ ; a colorless liquid; standard 350 ppm). Used for dry cleaning and to clean metals. In recent years it has largely replaced carbon tetrachloride for these purposes. Nearly 3 million workers are exposed to its seriously harmful effects. It can cause corneal burns, narcosis, and liver damage. Particularly large amounts depress the central nervous system, slow reaction time, and may even result in death. Also known as vinyl trichloride and methyl chloroform.

**TRICHLOROETHYLENE (TCE)** ($C_2 HCl_3$ ; a colorless sweet-smelling liquid; standard 100 ppm). Used chiefly as a solvent, especially in degreasing machine parts and in cleaning septic tanks; also in dry cleaning and in removing caffeine from coffee. The United States produces about 234,000 metric tons per year of this substance. An estimated 280,000 workers are exposed. TCE acts on the central nervous system and moderate exposure can cause symptoms similar to alcohol intoxication. It also has a toxic effect on the liver and kidneys, and can cause death due to irregular heart rhythm. Animal studies show that at large doses it causes cancer in mice. In 1976 the National Cancer Institute determined that TCE was carcinogenic and was found in the water supply, largely as a result of septic tank cleaning. The material has mostly been replaced by methylene chloride for removing the caffeine from coffee. (11)

## 2, 4, 5-TRICHLOROPHENOXYACETIC ACID (2,4,5-T)

($C_8 H_5 Cl_3 O_3$; a colorless odorless solid; standard 10 mg/m$^3$). A widely used herbicide that is now restricted to rice crops and rangelands. Between 1976 and 1978 the U.S. Forest Service sprayed forests around Orleans, California, with 2,4,5-T to remove brush and leafy plants. Of the 30 pregnant women in the area, 19 miscarried or gave birth to dead or deformed babies. Five of the children have cleft palate. In 1978 the substance was restricted on the possibility that it was carcinogenic, teratogenic, and fetotoxic. It is known to attack the skin, liver, and gastrointestinal tract. Animal studies show ataxia, skin irritations, rash, and blood in the stool. Where forests were sprayed, animals sickened and died; many birds disappeared. (11)

## TRINITROTOLUENE (TNT) (TNA) ($C_7 H_5 N_3 O_6$; colorless

crystals; standard 1.5 mg/m$^3$). Used as a high explosive. Upon absorption into the body it can irritate the eyes, nose, throat, cause sneezing and coughing, and lead to stained skin, hair, and nails. Excessive exposure to the dust, fumes, or vapor of this substance can cause fatal hepatitis or anemia, breathing difficulties, cataracts, weakness, muscle pains, heart irregularities, and neuritis.

## TRIS ($C_4 H_{11} NO_3$). Used as a flame retardant in textiles,

fabrics, clothing, furniture, toys, and wigs. Its full name is Tris (2,3-dibromopropyl) phosphate. The substance was widely used in sleepwear for children after Congress passed a law (1967) requiring that such garments be made fire-retardant. In 1977 a National Cancer Institute study documented cancer of the liver, kidney, lung, and stomach in mice caused by Tris. In humans, the substance is absorbed through the skin and attacks the central nervous system. The CPSC found that the substance was mutagenic. At risk were many millions of children and others. There are no data on a link between Tris and human cancer. In April 1977 the sale of Tris-treated garments was banned and all further production of the chemical for use in the United States was stopped. But shipments abroad continued until June 1978. Currently there is no further production or use of the substance. (11)

**TURPENTINE** ($C_{10}H_{16}$; a colorless flammable liquid; standard 100 ppm). A sticky mixture of resin and oil obtained from certain pine trees. It is used as a solvent, especially in thinning paints and varnishes. It is an irritating substance, and it can cause narcosis as well as damage to the kidneys. Low concentrations have been known to irritate the eyes, nose, and throat in individuals exposed. Acute intoxication from the vapors produces central nervous system depression with such symptoms as headache, nausea, confusion, and disturbed vision. Continued inhalation of the vapors can cause a chronic nephritis and a predisposition to pneumonia.

# U

**ULTRAVIOLET RADIATION.** Rays with wavelengths shorter than those of visible light and longer than those of X-rays. They are present in sunlight, welding arcs, and light from mercury-vapor lamps, for example. This radiation can have toxic effects upon the body. Farmers, sailors, arc welders, and others are affected by such eye and skin conditions as conjunctivitis, keratitis, and skin cancer.

**URANIUM** (U; a silver-white flammable element; standard 0.25 mg/m$^3$). A naturally radioactive element made up of 99.3 percent U$^{238}$, 0.7 percent U$^{235}$ and traces of U$^{234}$. Radiologists and miners, among others, are at risk from this most highly toxic substance. From animal experiments with uranium, scientists find that it produces cancer of the skin, lung, and bone, as well as leukemia. See also **RADIOACTIVE SUBSTANCES.**

**VC.** See **VINYL CHLORIDE.**

**VINYL CHLORIDE (VC)** (C$_2$H$_3$Cl; a flammable liquid with a pleasant etherlike odor; standard 1 ppm). A raw material used in about 50 factories around the country to produce plastic containers, wrapping film, floor tiles, furniture, table-cloths, phonograph records, electrical insulation, pipes, and other forms of polyvinyl chloride (PVC). Vinyl chloride is dangerous during manufacture. In 1970 scientists found that inhalation of VC by rats led to vascular and bone changes, and to cancer at very high doses. Four years later, the B.F. Goodrich Chemical Company informed NIOSH that four workers in their Louisville plant had died of a rare liver cancer, possibly related to VC exposure. Vinyl chloride was found to cause a cancer of the liver in humans that cannot be diagnosed until it is incurable. Severe exposure can cause central nervous system depression, with symptoms like drunkenness. Nearly 400,000 workers handle this substance and are at risk for liver, lung, brain, and kidney cancer. Also at risk are those living nearby. Currently the 1974 VC standard, banning use in aerosol sprays and limiting use in food packaging, is still in effect. The FDA, though, is considering removing the food packaging limit, since the manufacturers now claim the VC is a safer product. Also called chloroethylene. See also **POLY-VINYLCHLORIDE.** (51)

**VINYL CYANIDE.** See **ACRYLONITRILE.**

**VINYL TRICHLORIDE.** See **1,1,1-TRICHLOROETHANE.**

**WASTE OIL.** Already-used lubricating oil from automobile service stations. Waste oil presents a special environmental problem. It is ubiquitous and is also a potential carrier for other hazardous wastes and substances, such as PCBs and heavy metals. See also **TIMES BEACH, MISSOURI CHEMICALS** and **HEAVY METALS.**

**WINTERGREEN OIL.** See **METHYL SALICYLATE.**

**WOOD ALCOHOL.** See **METHANOL.**

**WOOD PRESERVATIVES.** Compounds that are used to protect wood from pests and rot. In 1985 the EPA banned the public sale of creosote, pentachlorophenol, and arsenicals, which were found to cause cancer and genetic defects in animals. Now only trained, certified people can buy these substances. Treated wood products, such as fences, sundecks, utility poles, lawn furniture, and railroad ties are available, but with instructions for safe handling. Pentachlorophenol contains an isomer of dioxin. EPA rules lowered the dioxin level in pentachlorophenol to 1 ppm. Currently, when creosote or pentachlorophenol is used on wood intended for human contact, it must be coated with shellac or another sealant. See also **ZINC CHLORIDE.**

**X-RAYS.** Electromagnetic radiation that can be extremely dangerous to living things. Radiologists as well as medical and dental workers are at risk from skin cancer and leukemia. Patients are also at risk. Americans receive a total of about 240 million medical and dental X-ray exams a year. No one knows how many cases of cancer result from this exposure, since it usually takes over 30 years for the cancer to appear.

**XYLENE** ($C_8H_{10}$; a colorless flammable liquid; 100 ppm). Used as a solvent (part of paint, ink, dyes, cements, cleaning fluids), and in the manufacture of plastics, synthetic textiles, perfumes, and drugs. Exposure to small amounts of the substance causes irritation of the eyes, nose, throat, and skin. Large doses of xylene cause central nervous system depression and liver and kidney damage.

# Y

**YELLOW 5, YELLOW 6.** See **FOOD COLORS.**

# Z

**ZINC CHLORIDE** ($ZnCl_2$; white crystalline solid; standard 1 mg/m$^3$). Used as a wood preservative, in dry cell batteries, and in oil refining. It is one of the most dangerous and toxic compounds of zinc. On contact it can cause damage to the eyes, skin, and mucous membranes. Inhalation of the substance can result in pain, swelling, and damage to the eyes.

# FOR FURTHER INFORMATION

## Government Agencies

Council on Environmental Quality
722 Jackson Place, NW
Washington, DC 20506

Environmental Protection Agency
401 M Street, SW
Washington, DC 20460

Food and Drug Administration
5600 Fishers Lane
Rockville, MD 20852

National Institute of Environmental Health Sciences
P.O. Box 12233
Research Triangle Park, NC 27709

National Toxicology Program
P.O. Box 12233
Research Triangle Park, NC 27709

Nuclear Regulatory Agency
1717 H Street, NW
Washington, DC 20555

Occupational Safety and Health Administration
200 Constitution Avenue, NW
Washington, DC 20210

Public Health Service
200 Independence Avenue, SW
Washington, DC 20201

## Consumer Organizations

Asbestos Victims of America
312 Essex Street
Gloucester City, NJ 08030

Environmental Action Foundation
724 Dupont Circle Building, NW
Washington, DC 20036

Environmental Defense Fund
1525 18th Street, NW
Washington, DC 20036

Natural Resources Defense Council
1350 New York Avenue, NW
Suite 300
Washington, DC 20005

Physicians for Social Responsibility
639 Massachusetts Avenue
Cambridge, MA 02139

Public Citizen Health Research Group
200 P Street, NW
Washington, DC 20036

## Industry Groups

Asbestos Information Association
1745 Jefferson Davis Highway
Arlington, VA 22202

Chemical Manufacturers Association
2501 M Street, NW
Washington, DC 20037

# REFERENCES

BOOKS

1. Brown, Michael. *Laying Waste*. New York: Washington Square Press, 1981.
2. Epstein, Samuel S. and Richard D. Grundy. *Consumer Health and Product Hazards*. Cambridge, MA: MIT Press, 1974.
3. Epstein, Samuel S., Lester O. Brown and Carl Pope. *Hazardous Waste in America*. San Francisco: Sierra Club, 1982.
4. Epstein, Samuel S. *The Politics of Cancer*. New York: Anchor Press/Doubleday, 1979.
5. Frick, G. William. *Environmental Glossary*. Washington, D.C.: Government Institutes, 1980.
6. Goldsmith, Frank and Lorin E. Kerr. *Occupational Safety and Health*. New York: Human Sciences Press, 1982.
7. National Institute for Occupational Safety and Health. *Registry of Toxic Effects of Chemical Substances*. Cincinnati: Department of Health and Human Services, 1983.
8. Null, Gary. *Body Pollution*. New York: Arco, 1973.
9. Odell, Rice. *Environmental Awakening*. New York: Harper, 1980.
10. Patrick, P.K. *Glossary on Solid Waste*. Copenhagen: World Health Organization, 1980.
11. Regenstein, Lewis. *America the Poisoned*. Washington, D.C.: Acropolis, 1982.

12. Sax, N. Irving and Benjamin Feiner. *Dangerous Properties of Industrial Materials.* New York: Van Nostrand Reinhold, 1984.

13. Sittig, Marshall. *Handbook of Toxic and Hazardous Chemicals.* Park Ridge, NJ: Noyes Publications, 1981.

14. Stewart, Richard B. and James E. Krier. *Environmental Law and Policy.* Indianapolis: Bobbs-Merrill, 1978.

## PAMPHLETS

### Conservation Foundation
15. Siting Hazardous Waste Management Facilities

### Environmental Protection Agency
16. Everybody's Problem: Hazardous Waste
17. Guidance for Controlling Friable Asbestos-Containing Materials in Buildings
18. Superfund: What it is, How it Works
19. Superfund's Remedial Response Program
20. Your Guide to the Environmental Protection Agency

### League of Women Voters
21. Blueprint for Clean Water
22. A Hazardous Waste Primer
23. A Nuclear Waste Primer

### National Institute for Occupational Safety and Health
24. Ethylene Dibromide
25. Ethylene Oxide
26. NIOSH Recommendations for Occupational Health Standards
27. Pocket Guide to Chemical Hazards

National Wildlife Federation
28. The Toxic Substances Dilemma
29. Toxic Substances Programs in U.S. States and Territories

Occupational Safety and Health Administration
30. Acrylonitrile Standard: Management's Role
31. Acrylonitrile: Worker Health Alert
32. Asbestos Standard: Management's Role
33. Asbestos: Worker Health Alert
34. Beryllium
35. Cancer in the Rubber Industry
36. Carbon Monoxide
37. Chemical Hazard Communication
38. Coke Oven Work and Cancer
39. Construction Industry
40. Cotton Dust: Worker Health Alert
41. General Industry
42. Health Hazards of Asbestos
43. Health Hazards of Inorganic Arsenic
44. Hearing Conservation
45. Hot Environments
46. Informing Workers and Employers about Occupational Cancer
47. Longshoring Industry
48. Mercury
49. Shipyard Industry
50. Toluene Diisocyanate
51. Vinyl Chloride

Public Health Service
52. Asbestos Exposure
53. National Toxicology Program